China and Africa Security

Fanie Herman

First edition, first print 2022

Independently published. Pretoria, South Africa.

goaf1023@gmail.com

Printed and bound by APub, Washington, USA.

ISBN 979-837-0101-168

Preface

China's pursuit of international security has increased significantly in recent years and Africa offers opportunities and challenges to achieve strategic and security goals. Political and military solidarity, the Belt and Road Initiative (BRI), the party-military model, the development-security complex, capacity-building, and peacekeeping missions are all dimensions of China's security involvement on the continent. The nature and scope of China's international security ambitions are enormous and the military is a tool to promote diplomacy. China-Africa military relations have changed dramatically, from support during the liberation struggle to training programs in the modern era. The attempt in this book is to cover the broad spectrum of China and African security to understand the relationship better.

Fanie Herman

Pretoria 2022

Table of Contents

List of Acronyms

AfCFTA = African Free Trade Area

AFRICOM = African Command Center

AIIB = Asian Infrastructure Investment Bank

ANC = African National Congress

AU = African Union

AVIC = Aviation Industry Corporation of China

GDP = Gross Domestic Product

BRICS = Brazil, Russia, India, China, South Africa

CAPSFZ = China-Africa Peace and Security Fund

CAR = Conflict Armament Research

CCP = Chinese Communist Party

CIPCC = China International Press Communication Center

CNPC = China National Petroleum Corporation

COMESA = Common Market for Eastern and Southern Africa

CRBC = China Roads and Bridges Corporation

DRC = Democratic Republic of the Congo

ECOWAS = Economic Community of West African States

EXIM = Export-Import Bank of China

FRELIMO = Liberation Front of Mozambique

FARDC = Military of the Democratic Republic of the Congo

FDLR = Democratic Forces for the Liberation of Uganda

FNLA = National Front for the Liberation of Angola

GNPOC = Greater Nile Petroleum Operating Company

IISS = International Institute for Strategic Studies

LAPSSET = Lamu-Port-South-Sudan-Ethiopia Transport

JEM = Justice Equality Movement

LRA = Lord's Resistance Army

MDS = Ministry of Public Security

MINUSMA = United Nations Multidimensional Integrated Stabilization Mission in Mali

MOD = Ministry of Defense

MOFA = Ministry of Foreign Affairs

MOFCOM = Ministry of Commerce

MONUSCO = United Nations Organization Stabilization Mission

MOOTW = Military Operations other than War

MPLA = People's Movement for the Liberation of Angola

M23 = March 23 Movement

NATO = North Atlantic Treaty Organization

NDRC = National Development and Reform Commission

NID = National Intelligence Service

NIF = National Islamic Front

NORINCO = China North Industries Corporation

NVS = National Security Strategy

PAC = Pan Africa Congress

PBoC = People's Bank of China

POLYTECH = Polytechnologies

RENAMO = Mozambican National Resistance

RMB = Rénmìnbì

RPG = Rocket Propelled Grenade

R2P = Responsibility to Protect

SADC = Southern African Development Community

SAR = Central African Republic

SCIO = State Council Information Office

SEZs = Special Economic Zones

SHADE = Shared Awareness and Deconfliction

SLM = Sudan Liberation Movement

SMK = Central Military Commission

SNSK = Central National Security Commission

SOK = Shanghai Development Corporation

SPLA = Sudan People's Liberation Army

SPLM-IO = Sudan's People's Liberation Movement-In Opposition

SSA = Sub-Saharan Africa

SSPDF = South Sudan's People's Defense Forces

SWAPO = Southwest Africa People's Organization

TAZARA = Tanzania-Zambia Railway

TPDF = Tanzania People's Defense Forces

UNAMID = United Nations African Mission in Darfur

UNITA = National Union for Total Independence of Angola

UNMEE = United Nations Mission in Ethiopia and Eritrea

UNMIL = United Nations Mission in Liberia

UNMISS = United Nations Mission in South Sudan

USSR = Union of Soviet Socialist Republics

UAE = United Arab Emirates

UN = United Nations

WHO = World Health Organization

ZANLA = Zimbabwe African National Liberation Military

ZANU-PF = Zimbabwe African National Liberation Union

ZAPU = Zimbabwe African People's Union

ZELA = Zimbabwe Environmental Law Association

ZTE = Zhongxing Telecommunication Equipment Corporation

Chapter 1 : Introduction

Not much is known about China's ancient relationship with Africa, although there is evidence of early trade contacts. Highlights of medieval contacts include the visit of the Moroccan traveler and academic, Ibn Battuta to China in the 1400s, the visit of the Somali traveler and academic Sa'id to China in the 1400s and the visit of the seafarer Zheng He to the east coast of Africa in the 1500s. Zheng He explored lands in the west at the request of Emperor Ming. Furthermore, beads made of glass and porcelain were found at the large Zimbabwean ruins.

Modern relations between China and Africa date back to the era of Mao Zedong. The Chinese Communist Party (CCP) defeated the nationalist forces in the Chinese Revolution and proclaimed the People's Republic of China (PRC), in 1949. Mao supported freedom movements in Africa in their struggle for independence. It was primarily aimed at bringing colonialism and Western imperialism to an end. Furthermore, relations were established with countries that followed the ideology of communism.

The central theme of the book is about China's military diplomacy and dimensions of security in Africa. China has begun to display more assertive and aggressive international behavior in the last decade. This is due to the country's expansion of political, economic and military power in the international political arena and the pursuit of great power status. The driving force behind the rise of China is the revival of Chinese nationalism and the focus on socialism with Chinese characteristics. These concepts actually date back to the earlier years of the Chinese Revolution and were advocated by Chinese leaders to unite the country.

With the takeover of Xi Jinping in 2013, the ideas went into effect and were officially incorporated as part of China's foreign policy. The maintaining of sovereignty means that security also has to be strengthened. Security goes hand in hand with the revival of nationalism and economic development and is a key focus area of the country's domestic and foreign policy. A new concept has been formulated that perceives and interprets all aspects of Chinese society, including, politics, economics, social, cultural, education and technology through the lens of security. Xi Jinping refers to it as China's new comprehensive security concept. External threats are now being assessed on the basis of the impact they have on internal threats, such as Western countries' criticism of Chinese security legislation in Hong Kong and the monitoring of Chinese citizens abroad against the CCP's policy at home. Economic diplomacy is the main driver of China's relations with African countries. Infrastructure building, investment in major projects and economic development are among the initiatives. On the other hand, energy diplomacy also plays a big role. This refers to the acquisition of oil, gas and minerals to keep China's economic machine running.

There are also forms of soft power, for example teaching Mandarin at Confucian centers, cultural exchange shows and academic exchange programs that are very popular. The Chinese government offers hundreds of scholarships for African students to study in China every year. The establishment of telecommunications networks and sharing of information technology has also increased in the last few years.

In 1954, the Five Principles of Peaceful Coexistence were formulated, which was a guide for China's foreign policy with other countries. It took place under the rule of Mao ZeDong. The principles include, mutual respect for sovereignty and territorial integrity, mutual non-aggression, non-interference in the domestic affairs of other countries, equality and mutual benefit and peaceful coexistence. This was at a time when China was reaching out to non-communist countries in Asia to establish friendly and diplomatic relations.

The principles stipulated that there would be no interference in the countries' domestic affairs. Countries in Southeast Asia, for example Malaysia and Singapore gained independence during the period, while other countries, for example, Vietnam and Lagos were involved in military conflicts. The Chinese leadership believed that countries should have the ability to solve their own internal problems.

The principles were also applied to Africa. African countries after independence had to be given the opportunity to develop their own economies without the interference of foreign powers. For about three decades, China provided only financial and military aid, without interfering in African countries' domestic affairs. During the Cold War years, Russia dominated the communist narrative in Africa, which significantly diminished China's influence. An overview of China's foreign policy and diplomacy is discussed in Chapter 2.

Xi Jinping 's goal of giving the Chinese military greater international influence took shape during the 19th National Congress of the CCP in October 2017. Xi stated that the Chinese military needs to be transformed into a world-class military that can execute the party's policies, that can win wars, and that can maintain a professional, international status. By 2049, China must be a modern, strong, culturally educated and harmonious community. At the same time, China must be able to protect its international interests from terrorist attacks, public unrest, anti-Chinese sentiments, as well as local expectations that Beijing will act to protect the interests of citizens.

Security needs to be especially sharpened in countries where Chinese citizens work, for example on Belt and Road Initiative (BRI) routes. China's pursuit of international security is discussed in Chapter 3.

China's military diplomacy with Africa spans many decades and is divided into several periods. During these periods, different strategies and policies were formulated to promote military relations.

With the onset of the 21st century, China's military diplomacy in Africa has taken a new turn. Training programs are offered, visits by high-ranking military officers to African armies, visits by naval vessels to African ports, for example visits by the Chinese hospital ship (the peace arc) to conflict areas around Africa's coast. This ship provides medical assistance and humanitarian aid. Participation in peacekeeping missions also increases China's reputation in African countries. Then there are joint military exercises with African armies to improve mobility and gain experience.

The first China-Africa Defense Security Forum took place in 2018. Senior military officers from 49 African countries and the African Union (AU) attended the forum in Beijing. Various issues were addressed, such as regional security, military cooperation and cooperation with civil protection units for the security of facilities and civilians. A forum for the training of law enforcers was also held in 2018.

China's Africa policy document of 2015 proposed that hundreds of African military personnel be sent to China to undergo training. The Ministry of Defense further planned to offer workshops in logistics management, healthcare, humanitarian aid and rescue operations. The strategic and policy aspects of China's military diplomacy with African countries are discussed in Chapter 4.

In the early 2000s, troops were deployed to the United Nations peacekeeping mission in the Democratic Republic of Congo (DRC). This was the first indication that China was prepared to become involved in Africa's security. Security here refers to instability and conflict, the protection of civilians, the security of facilities and oil refineries, the provision of personnel and technology to protect trade routes and economic networks, and the installation of detection systems.

Broadly speaking, China's involvement in Africa's security differs from the country's forms of military diplomacy. China initially followed the traditional way of peacekeeping, which stipulates, among other things, that participating countries may not interfere in conflict between the warring factions. This is in line with the Five Principles of Peaceful Coexistence. As the challenges of peacekeeping have changed, the traditional way has been combined with other means of peacekeeping, such as building peace and sending police officers to maintain law and order. Participation in peacekeeping missions are discussed in Chapter 5.

China's arms sales to African countries have grown significantly in the last decade. In the earlier years of the relationship, mainly light weapons and ammunition were provided to liberation movements in the struggle for independence and there was rivalry between China and Russia for weapon supplies to African liberation movements. The decision to supply weapons was also based on different interpretations of the communist ideology. Would it be Marxist-Leninism as applied in Russia or Mao Ze Dong's adaptation of the latter school of thought. African countries with socialist governments at that time received larger financial loans and weapons from Russia. China did supply arms to Angola, Mozambique, Tanzania and Mozambique on a much smaller scale.

The party-military model introduced by Mao ZeDong stipulates that the party controls the military and the military may never be allowed to control the party. The armies of most African countries are legitimate, autonomous institutions that has a constitutional function to protect the country's borders. Armies also perform functions, such as, emergency control in times of unrest and humanitarian assistance in times of natural disasters. In general, armies in Africa are institutions with their own rules, regulations and procedures and not tools in the hands of the ruling party to pursue political, economic and military goals. Observers of African politics are concerned that the Chinese party-military model could be detrimental to the relationship between the citizens and the ruling party.

Capacity building is a further dimension of China's involvement in Africa's security. African governments in some respects are experiencing similar security problems as in China, for example, poverty, discrimination, underdevelopment and instability. These problems make them natural partners with China. Furthermore, cooperation and capacity building facilitate the institutionalization of norms, values and shared interests in multilateral forums. Examples here are the China-Africa Peace Security Partnership, which was established in 2012 and the forerunner to the 2018 China-Africa Peace Security Forum.

The development-security complex describes the Chinese government's view that development is an essential element for the establishment of security. China's investments in capacity building programs are currently part and parcel of sustainable peace and security in Africa. Leaders in China believe that investing in human resources will result in economic development. This in turn creates a stable and safe environment. Chinese security contractors currently play an important role in protecting Chinese facilities and citizens in Africa. This industry is controlled by the state. By law, agents of the CCP must serve on the board of private security companies before guards can be hired. These guards are trained to protect China's property and facilities. While it is true that smaller Chinese businesses use local security contractors, they do not enjoy state protection if contractual, labor, and labor disputes occur. These smaller companies have to take care of their own legal obligations. Arms sales, the party-military model, the development-security complex and the role of security contractors are discussed in Chapter 6.

China's GPI is a comprehensive, economic development project that seeks to connect China with the heartland of Europe. The goal is to facilitate the flow of goods and services on China's rural and maritime routes. The project has also been extended to Africa, where infrastructure is being built at enormous cost. Funding for the projects are mostly acquired from Chinese State Banks and the Asian Development Bank. There are also hundreds of private companies advancing money for the development projects. Most Chinese immigrants in Africa are involved in GPI projects and other projects funded by Chinese banks.

Various action plans are developed to address BRI-related challenges. These include anti-terrorism assistance, law enforcement, early warning systems, infrastructure security and traditional military assistance. The BRI's centrality to China's global strategy assumes that involvement in Africa's security will increase. Furthermore, the BRI was developed to be compatible with the AU's Agenda 2063. The AU's Agenda 2063 is a strategic framework for the socio-economic transformation of Africa over the next 50 years. It builds and seeks to accelerate the implementation of previous and existing growth and development initiatives. There is also talk that China is trying to link the BRI to The African Continental Free Trade Area (AcFTA) which came into force in 2020. The BRI is discussed in Chapter 7.

During the 1955 Bandung Conference in Indonesia, Mao Ze Dong pledged his support to African countries in their struggle for independence. This Chinese leader was aware that an anti-colonial and anti-imperialist agenda would liberate Africa from Western domination and proclaimed himself as the natural leader of liberation movements. The motivation was measured by the success that Mao's communist troops achieved against nationalist forces in the Chinese revolution. Weapons and ammunition were supplied to countries in Africa that fought against Western imperialism and colonialism. In the modern era, however, arms are supplied to almost every African country based on commercial purposes and where strong political solidarity exists. There are also claims that China is exchanging weapons for natural resources. Angola, the DRC, Mozambique, Sudan, South Sudan, Tanzania, Zambia, and Zimbabwe are discussed as case studies in Chapter 8.

China will continue to maintain bilateral relations with African governments. The political, economic and social capital invested in the last two decades have brought about major changes in the relationship. The acquisition of natural resources is important to keep China's economic machine going, the signing of partnerships is important to exert strategic influence, the variety of multilateral forums is important to negotiate matters of common interest and the sale of arms is important to promote military diplomacy. A summary of all the dimensions and aspects of China's security in Africa is discussed in Chapter 9.

Chapter 2 : Diplomatic Overview and Foreign Policy

The origins of modern human civilization can be found in both China and Africa. In both areas, positive contributions have been made to the social development of man. Although separated by the Indian and parts of the Pacific Oceans, the friendship has existed since ancient times. Anthropologists claim that the first contact between the two civilizations dates back to the 14th century, when the Chinese seafarer, Zheng He, landed on the east coast of Africa in present-day Kenya. The Western historian Teobaldo Filesi wrote in his book "China and Africa in the Middle Ages" that the purpose of the visit was to forge friendly ties between the nations of Africa and China.[1]

The establishment of the PRC in 1949 led to a new chapter in China-Africa relations. In the 1950s and 1960s, a large number of African countries gained independence and decided to establish diplomatic relations with China. During Deng Xiaoping 's visit to Africa, he emphasized the importance of solidarity and the establishment of bilateral relations.[2] In 1960, Mao Zedong received a delegation from 12 African countries and pledged China's unconditional support to those countries.[3] He also praised the countries in their struggle for freedom and anti-colonialism[4]

In 1974, Mao Zedong met Kenneth Kaunda, the leader of Zambia and introduced his theory of three worlds. The theory advocates three political-economic worlds: the first world, the second world and the third world. The first world consists of America and the Soviet Union; the two great powers with imperialist motives. The second world consists of Japan, Canada, Europe and other countries of the global north. The third world consists of Africa, Latin America and continental Asia.[5] Deng Xiaoping presented the theory to the UN General Assembly in 1974, pointing to the difficulties China is facing to obtain raw materials for the country's economy. Deng accused western countries of dominating the production and supply of raw materials, thereby making poorer countries dependent on western supply chains.[6]

This situation strained relations with non-communist countries and continued until after the end of the Cold War.[7] Prime Minister Zhou Enlai (1949-1976) visited Africa three times in the 1960s to promote bilateral relations. During his visits, time was spent on developing programs to assist African countries economically. During a state visit by Zhou Enlai to Ghana in 1964, eight foreign policy principles were formulated that served as a guide to establish relations with other countries. The eight principles are as follows:

1) Future assistance will be based on the principle of equality and mutual benefit.

2) The Chinese government provides the aid without reservation and respects the sovereignty of countries receiving the aid.

3) China provides economic assistance in the form of interest-free or low interest loans and is flexible to repayments.

4) China does not desire to place recipients in a dependent position, but encourages other countries to become self-sufficient and stimulate economic growth.

5) The Chinese government will help other countries to build infrastructure and invest for economic growth.

6) The Chinese government will provide equipment and materials based on international accepted standards.

7) The Chinese government will ensure that training programs and technical assistance are provided to the countries.

8) Experts tasked with training and management of projects will adapt to the living standards of the recipient countries and not impose the Chinese way of life on local populations. The laws of the land will be obeyed and the rules followed.[8]

Deng Xiaoping , in his term as leader of China, devoted much time to looking after the development and prosperity of China's friends. During his meetings with Presidents Nyerere of Kenya, Chissano of Mozambique, Dos Santos of Angola, Mugabe of Zimbabwe and Museweni of Uganda, China's experience in revolutionary warfare was shared with these leaders. Deng urged African countries to look for political systems that are favorable to their own situations and not indiscriminately follow other countries' systems.[9]

Jiang Zemin , visited Africa four times and made a number of proposals to strengthen China-Africa relations in the new era. [10]The new era refers to the early 1990s with the announcement of China's going out policy. Attempts have been made to reach abroad for the conclusion of strategic partnerships and the introduction of China's economy to the world.[11]

Diplomatic Overview

China's Foreign Ministry has put in place a variety of mechanisms to promote dialogue with African governments. This includes support for the One-China Policy. [12] China and African countries have launched various programs to promote visits and ideological solidarity. Mutual support in international affairs is also on the agenda, for example human rights issues or non-support for military intervention in war-torn and conflict areas of the world. In the multilateral forums, joint efforts are being made to protect the rights of developing countries and to push for the creation of a new and just political and economic world order. The Forum for China-Africa Cooperation (FOCAC), currently serves as a good example where China and Africa are negotiating common issues. The forum was established in 2000.

China has helped develop African countries economically since independence. While continuing to offer economic aid, private companies and entrepreneurs are encouraged to invest in Africa. There is also collaboration in education and training, public health care, culture and other fields of interest. Scholarships are offered to students from

Africa and various student recruitment campaigns are launched each year.[13]

China initially had sound relations with the African National Congress (ANC) during the freedom struggle.[14] As China's relations with the Soviet Union weakened during the Cold War years and the ANC moved closer to the Soviet Union, the Chinese leadership decided to support the Pan-Africa Congress (PAC).[15]

China's military relations with African countries date back to the Cold War years. It was a period in which China was willing to support freedom movements in the struggle for independence. Political allies included Somalia and Tanzania and military relations included Egypt and Algeria.[16] Military equipment worth 142 million USD was sold to African countries between 1955 and 1977.[17]

The ideology of the CCP has undergone dramatic changes over the years. Especially during the tenure of Deng Xiaoping and the current president Xi Jinping. While some experts claim that the CCP shows a lack of direction, the ideology of the CCP is still based on communism. Nationalism was an important ideological tool of the CCP to unite Chinese language and culture and used especially during the Cultural Revolution. [18] Local populations identified with the populist nature of Chinese leaders and the principles and ideals of the CCP. The Chinese Revolution of 1911 served as a prelude to the rise of revolutionary leaders such as Mao Zedong, Zhou Enlai, and Hua Guofeng.[19] These leaders all played a prominent role in the establishment of the PRC. Marxism on the one hand was a spiritual utopia for early communist leaders and on the other hand leaders used Marxism as a foundation for the spread of the communist ideology. The amalgamation of the different ideological views was put into practise during the CCP's Great Social and Economic Campaign.[20]

The argument in recent years is that the CCP no longer uses ideology as a basis for governing; the party acts more pragmatically and only implement policies that works in practise. Officials in the party, however, have different views. Former President Hu Jintao, for example, declared in 2012 that the West was trying to divide China. The international culture of the West is strong, while the culture of China is weak. Party schools are now tasked with promoting culture among the population.[21]

Chinese leaders believed that stagnation of the communist ideology was one of the reasons for the dissolution of the Soviet Union.[22] Officials in the CCP further argues that party ideology should be dynamic. This will ensure the survival of the party. In the Soviet Union, ideology became rigid, unimaginative, and disconnected from reality.[23]

President Xi Jinping, in a speech held in 2012, stated that the ideals and beliefs of the CCP are the foundations on which the Chinese state and nation are built. If the population doubts these ideals and beliefs, a Chinese community with socialist characteristics cannot be established. Therefore, it is necessary to connect the ideals and beliefs of the masses with the party. In this way, China will achieve victories in every area of life.[24]

Since the breakup of the Soviet Union, the main spiritual values of members have become more prominent. This is viewed in the light of the growth of capitalism after the end of the Cold War. Xi Jinping believes that a lack of insights from party members into the ideals and beliefs of the CCP, are responsible for increased corruption and misconduct. Xia Minghan, one of the former leaders of the Chinese revolution, stated that loyal followers of the revolution do not have to be afraid of arrest and possible execution, as long as they only believe in "ism". This suffix refers to communism as a system or philosophy that is often portrayed in a political way or as part of a political movement. Fang Zhimin, who was known for gueurilla attacks against the regime of Chiang-Kai-Shek's Nationalist Party, stated: "The enemy can take us prisoner and kill us, but will never change our political beliefs." These revolutionaries firmly believed in the ideals and principles of communism and served as role models for emerging leaders of the CCP.[25]

Hu Jintao proposed the formulation of a new value system for the CCP. He referred to the new system as socialism with Chinese characteristics. Hu stated in his speech that Marxism is still the leading ideology of the CCP and that nationalism and patriotism should serve as the basis for a socialist value system. It is the task of the CCP to integrate the core values of socialism in all spheres of society.[26]

The Tenets of China's Foreign Policy

The core of China's foreign policy is summarized in the Five Principles of Peaceful Coexistence. These include respect for the sovereignty and territorial integrity of other countries, an approach of non-aggression to bilateral relations, non-interference in the domestic affairs of other countries, equal treatment of all nations and races, mutual benefit in economic negotiations and the peaceful coexistence of all countries on earth. Mao Zedong used the principles as guidelines to establish relations with countries in Asia.[27]

The principles were first used in an agreement between China and India dating back to 1954. The agreement was signed at that time by China, India and the Tibet region to strengthen trade ties. According to historians, the principles have their unofficial origin in the Sanskrit language or Panchsheel, where Panch refers to five and sheel to virtues, in other words the five virtues.[28]

The Indian diplomat, VV Paranjpe an expert in the field of China-Indian relations, argues that the principles of Panchsheel were officially formulated by Zhou Enlai, the Chinese Prime Minister during the reign of Mao Zedong. With the acceptance of the Indian delegation on 31 December 1953 to promote trade ties with Tibet, Zhou stated that China would use the five principles to give direction to China's relations with other countries. India's Prime Minister Jawaharlal Nehru supported the principles in a public speech only a few days after the signing of the

China-India Agreement. Nehru further argued that the principles should serve as a guide to determine friendly relations between all countries. As a further measure, the principles will help prevent wars and conflict. The Panchsheel Agreement served as one of the most important foundations for building China-Indian relations.[29]

In the recent past, Chinese presidents have referred to the principles as follows. In his meeting with President Bill Clinton in 1993, Jiang Zemin (1989-2002) pointed out the importance of these principles in strengthening US-Chinese bilateral relations. Hu Jintao (2002-2012) highlighted the contribution of these principles to achieving international peace and development during his speech before the United Nations (UN) General Assembly in 2005. Xi Jinping in a meeting with the leaders of Brazil, Russia, India and South Africa (BRICS) have noted that the Panchsheel Agreement is as relevant today as when it was signed in 1954.[30] During the 50th anniversary of the Panchsheel Agreement in 2004, the Chinese Foreign Ministry stated that a new international order must be built on the basis of the Five Principles.[31]

Chinese Prime Minister Wen Jiabao during the same event also said that China has established diplomatic relations with 165 countries since the signing of the agreement. Economic, cultural, technological and scientific exchange agreements have also been signed with 200 countries and regions. On the basis of the Panchsheel Agreement, it was possible for China to resolve border disputes and maintain peaceful relations with neighboring countries. Furthermore, China has managed to provide economic and technological aid to friends without any political favors.[32]

In June 2014, the Vice President of India was welcomed in the Boardroom of the CCP in Beijing for the 60th anniversary of the Panchsheel Agreement. In 2017, Xi Jinping stated that China would use the agreement as a signpost to promote cooperation with India.[33]

Shortly after the establishment of the PRC, Mao Zedong declared that China was ready to enter into diplomatic relations with countries that supported and accepted the principles of equality, mutual benefit and respect for territorial integrity and sovereignty. These principles were adopted at the First Session of the National Congress on September 29, 1949. The newly established PRC adopted the five principles as an embodiment of Chinas pursuit of peace and a harmonious coexistence with other countries. India and Burma are neighboring countries of China. Not only do their social systems differ from each other, but there are also historical disputes that have not yet been resolved. During the period of British colonial rule, Britain used territory in India to expand its influence into Tibet. The Qing dynasty of China granted special privileges to the British colonial power to impose discriminatory laws in Tibet. These include, slave trade, discriminatory and unequal treatment of Indian and Tibetan workers, and disregard for Tibetan labor rules and regulations.

This led to a trading system that benefited Britain's economy, but detrimental to economic growth in the rest of the Tibetan region. After the establishment of diplomatic relations between China and India in 1950, India hoped that it could receive the same benefits from China as Britain received from Tibet. However, the communist government of Mao Zedong insisted that all the privileges that India enjoyed in Tibet be revoked. The Chinese government decided to maintain the general rules and procedures that applied in Tibet. The needs of the population were also considered to find a solution to the dispute. The condition, however, was that China would not relinquish its sovereignty in Tibet, for the sake of better relations with the Tibetan people. In a spirit of good neighborliness and guided by the policy of reconciliation, China agreed to meet with India for a solution to the Tibet issue. The talks lasted from 31 December 1953 to 29 April 1954.[34]

Prime Minister Zhou Enlai met with officials of the Indian Parliament on 31 December 1953, where he introduced for the first time the Five Principles of Peaceful Coexistence. The Indian delegation agreed that the principles should be used as guidelines for the negotiations. The principles were included in the preamble to the agreement between the PRC and the Republic of India. The principles would henceforth serve as the norms that determine the relations between the two countries.

After protests against communist governments evolved in Europe in the 1950s, China promoted the principles along with the ideology of socialism abroad. The principles were in contradiction to power politics, which was a feature of western countries' approach to cooperation and conflict resolution in the Cold War years. The Five Principles of

Peaceful Coexistence have become the basic norms for the development of interstate relationships and transcend social systems and ideologies. The principles have been accepted by the majority of states in the world.[35] Benefits arising from the principles are an eradication of inequalities and discriminatory policies in economics and trade, a narrowing of gaps that exist in the development between rich and poor countries and the pursuit of common prosperity.[36]

A concept that stems from the principles is the building of a community with a shared future for humanity. The Chinese government promotes this concept to promote cooperation between developing countries. The concept means that all countries have equal sovereignty, no country can interfere in the domestic affairs of other countries, countries should work together to find solutions to international conflicts and disputes, countries should work together for win-win results and countries should strive for the amalgamation of diverse cultures and nations.[37]

Although China has made progress in terms of economic and technological development and the middle class is well established, the pace of progress is too slow.

Entering into partnerships with developing countries can speed up the pace, as both China and developing countries pursue common development.

China's position is that international disputes are resolved through peaceful negotiations. This is the position on the conflict in Afghanistan, Iraq, Syria, Palestine, Eastern Europe and Africa. This also includes other areas of the world where conflict is indicative of political, religious and border disputes. In the UN General Assembly, China does not participate in voting that authorizes the implementation of sanctions.

This is a matter of principle in conjunction with the Five Principles of Peaceful Coexistence. Furthermore, China does not support any resolutions for intervening in countries' internal conflicts, if it does not consider one or more of the Five Principles of Peaceful Coexistence. China is a permanent member of the UN Security Council and a negative vote amounts to a veto. In the past, China casted abstention votes or did not vote at all. This has led to several interventions that have been implemented without a reversal of China's commitment to non-interference.[38]

In recent times there are deviations or total disregard of the principles depending on political and strategic outcomes. For example, in China's claims to territory in the South China Sea, the principle of non-aggression is disregarded because military means are increasingly used to intimidate other countries. The principle of mutual benefit in economic negotiations with America are rhetorical and only benefits China's selfish economic, technological and digital dominance in the region.

In Africa, the principles are applied as widely as possible to maintain solidarity and friendly relations. However, there are certain cases, such as during the civil wars in the Sudanese where China intervened to protect oil interests. Maintaining sovereignty and respect for equality between states are principles that are non-negotiable. The further away from home China's interests are, the easier it is for the Chinese government to reconcile the principles with interests. On the other hand, the principles will remain at the heart of China's foreign policy, even with the many challenges in the international political arena.[39]

Xi Jinping's foreign policy refers to China's policy towards other countries. Xi Jinping succeeded Hu Jintao as

General Secretary of the CCP in 2012.[40] A feature of Xi's leadership is his focus on international security and the way in which it determines China's foreign policy. Xi projects a more nationalistic and assertive China on the world stage through the expansion of the Chinese value system and political structure. Within the ranks of the CCP there are opposing views to Xi's foreign policy, which has led Xi to embark on a massive restructuring of party policy.[41]

The rise of wolf warrior diplomacy is one of the results of this restructuring. Wolf warrior diplomacy gives Chinese diplomats more freedom to act aggressively in negotiations with diplomats from other countries. Wolf Warrior diplomacy is competitive and challenging. Xi Jinping's great power diplomacy is an attempt to expand China's international power and places China in direct ideological competition with the West.[42]

According to Wang Yi, China's foreign minister, Xi Jinping's thinking about diplomacy points to the reaching of a milestone in China's diplomatic history. The focus on superpower diplomacy has replaced Deng Xiaoping's earlier slogan of hiding your country's capabilities, buying time, and maintaining a low profile. In the first five years of Xi's leadership, the budget for diplomacy doubled. From 2020, Xi's great power diploma is taught as a subject in high schools and tertiary institutions.[43]

Foreign observers claim that Xi's way of thinking about diplomacy gives China the right to follow a different set of rules in international politics. However, Chinese citizens back home do not have a problem with Xi's way of thinking and view it in a positive light, especially citizens who have strong nationalist beliefs. In terms of theory, there are similarities to Mao Zedong's international relations theory, specifically the theory of three worlds. The theory of three worlds was proposed by Mao Zedong to the President of Algeria, Houari Boumédiène, in 1974. The first world consists of the United States and the Soviet Union.

The two countries are great powers and follow imperialist policies. The second world consists of Japan, Canada, Europe and other rich countries of the global north. The third world consists of China, countries in Africa, South America and continental Asia. From a scientific point of view, the three worlds theory is an interpretation of Mao's international perspective and a geopolitical reformulation of international relations.[44] This interpretation of Mao differs from the demographer Alfred Sauvy's three-world model. In Sauvy's model, the first world consists of America, the United Kingdom (UK) and their allies. The second world consists of the Russia, China and their allies. The third world consists of the economically, underdeveloped countries and the 120 countries of the non-allied movement (NAM).

Since 1949 official documentation of the CCP refers to this way of thinking, which is in actual fact a continuation of Marxism, Leninism, Mao's way of thinking, Deng Xiaoping's theory, Jiang Zemin's theory of three representatives, and Hu Jintao's Scientific Development Model. These thought processes are all part of a series on socialism that developed after the establishment of the PRC.

Maoism or Mao Zedong's way of thinking encompasses a variety of principles of Marx and Lenin that Mao developed to initiate a socialist revolution in the agricultural and pre-industrial community of China. The philosophical difference between Maoism and traditional Marxism-Leninism is that peasants or the farming community are the revolutionary vanguard in pre-industrial communities. In the Soviet Union, it was the masses. In modern China workers still adhere to Maoist principles to protect them from unfair labour practises and exploitation by large commercial farmers. From the 1950s until the economic reforms of Deng Xiaoping in the late 1970s, Maoism was the political and military ideology of the CCP. Revolutionary movements around the world followed Maoism in their struggles for freedom and independence.[45]

After the Sino-Soviet split of the 1960s, the CCP and the Communist Party of the Soviet Union attempted to use Marxism-Leninism to unite the masses and garner international support. There was also a struggle between the USSR and China over which country is the leader of communism in the world.[46]

Deng Xiaoping's theory was a series of political and economic principles with the goal to apply Marxism-Leninism and Maoism to the existing socio-economic situations in China. Deng's statement that facts are derived from truth was an important indicator of China's economic growth in subsequent decades.[47] Deng followed a pragmatic approach to implementing the CCP's economic policy. Socialism with Chinese characteristics was at the heart of Deng's way of thinking. In practise it meant the following. 1) The liberation and development of the workforce. 2) The elimination of exploitation and polarization of the workforce. 3) The pursuit of prosperity for all workers. Deng also proposed the four modernizations of the country's productive sectors. These include agriculture, industry, science and technology and the military.

The success of this modernization campaign depended on four cardinal principles. 1) Marxism-Leninism and Mao Zedong's way of thinking. 2) Socialism. 3) Authoritarian government and dictatorship and finally, leadership by the CCP. In terms of foreign policy, Deng began to open China to the world in the late 1970s. Special Economic Zones (SEZs) were established in Southeast Asian countries such as Vietnam, Myanmar, Laos and Cambodia. The aim was to promote trade with China. These countries all had communist governments at the time. China also exported agricultural products and heavy machinery to neighboring countries and competed with Western countries for economic influence.[48]

Jiang Zemin's theory of three representatives was introduced and ratified during the 16th Congress of the CCP in 2002. The three representatives defines the CCP's national policy and emphasizes that the party must always be in control of China's manufacturing process, the party must always ensure that China's culture is promoted and the party must always take the interests of Chinese citizens at heart. Hu Jintao, (2003-2012), introduced a new approach to ensure the progress of the Chinese nation. The Scientific Development Model was developed as a leading socio-economic indicator of the CCP.

This model utilizes scientific socialism, sustainable development, social development, peaceful coexistence and socialism with Chinese characteristics to bring about a better Chinese society. The model was ratified at the 17th Congress of the CCP in October 2007 and is viewed as an extension of Marxism-Leninism, Mao Zedong's thinking, the theory of Deng Xiaoping and Jiang Zemin's three representatives.[49]

Socialism with Chinese characteristics provides context to the implementation of China's foreign policy. Since Xi Jinping took office, the focus is on promoting socialism with Chinese characteristics. Yang Jiechi, China's top diplomat, claims that socialism with Chinese characteristics is the heart and soul of China's foreign policy and contributes to the sharing of knowledge and programs. Yang Jiechi also stated that a complete implementation of socialism with Chinese characteristics can solve humanity's problems. This theory creates context for concepts and principles of diplomatic relations. Peaceful development based on mutual respect, cooperation and benefit, for example, is a central theme of this theory.[50]

Chinese leaders believe that economic and security goals can be achieved if a community with a shared future for humanity is established. The first step is to pursue world peace and help countries develop economically before such a community can be established. The CCP is aware that goals cannot be achieved in isolation and seeks to involve all countries in China's diplomatic framework. If all countries are willing to work with China, it can bring peace, prosperity and prosperity to the entire international community.

China identifies four types of role players within the context of the new great power diplomacy. The four types are superpowers, neighboring countries, developing countries and international organizations. With regard to great powers, it is necessary to enter into stable and balanced relations within the multipolar system. With regard to neighboring countries, it is necessary to create a friendly and safe environment that can protect Beijing's interests and those of neighboring countries. With regard to developing countries, it is necessary to promote solidarity and cooperation. With regard to international organizations, it is necessary to promote diplomacy in the World Health Organization (WHO), the International Telecommunication Union (ITU), the Food and Agriculture Organization (FAO), as well as other organizations. Furthermore, the establishment of new types of bilateral and multilateral relations between states is an important element of the new diplomatic framework.

The concepts of mutual respect, cooperation and benefit form the basis for the new types of relationships. Yang Jiechi describes the relationships as strategic partnerships that spell out a new course of state-to-state or nation-to-nation interaction. The partnerships meet criteria such as law and equality, non-interference, non-aggression, respect for sovereignty and territorial independence. This leads to a higher level of bilateral relations. Diplomatic relations are further advanced with the establishment of comprehensive strategic partnerships, which unite the interests of partners in a geographical region. One important consequence is the pursuit of common economic and security goals.[51]

Government systems around the world are changing. This is an area where China is actively participating in developing a more balanced international system. The concept of a community with a shared future for humanity is especially promoted on BRI routes. The idea is to unite countries on the routes and bring them in harmony with the goals and ambitions of China. Furthermore, the BRI strengthens China's strategic partnerships, expands its network of strategic partners and helps with reforms of the international system.

China continues to expand its diplomatic footprint.

By the end of 2020, China had established formal diplomatic relations with 180 countries, including countries that shifted diplomatic relations from Taiwan to China. In addition, strategic partnerships have been established with 100 countries. By the end of 2019, Xi Jinping had visited 12 countries and attended several major international conferences. A number of diplomatic events took place in China in 2019, including the second

BRI International Cooperation Forum, where Xi acted as guest speaker.[52]

The Role of the CCP

The Communist Party is the ruling party of China that governs legally according to the constitution. The party gained legitimacy through the mass-line campaign instituted by Mao Zedong during the Chinese Revolution. The main element of the mass line is to gather information from the population, interpret the information through the lens of Marxism-Leninism and then implement it through policy. Mao developed the mass line into a methodology that summarizes philosophy, strategy, tactics, leadership, and organizational theory. A correct mass line is essential for the full consolidation of power. Xi Jinping and his colleagues acknowledge that there are many challenges which test the legitimacy of the CCP, especially those of corrupt party members.

According to Xi, the problems can be addressed in two ways. First, discipline, loyalty and the introduction of anti-corruption campaigns to remove unwanted elements from the party must be introduced. This will strengthen the party structures. Second, the mass-line campaign must be re-launched to bring party members into contact with ordinary citizens. Xi believes in the CCP as the main body for political control. The party's central bodies (Politburo and Central Military Commission) should exercise full control over all the party's activities.[53]

There is also considerable criticism of the current power and influence of the CCP. According to a report by the US government, the CCP poses the greatest threat to the continued existence of the current international norms and value system. The party undermines international stability to satisfy its own interests and hegemonic ambitions. Despite efforts to pursue development and peace, the party's policies and goals are detrimental to international cooperation and progress. In the economic field, the CCP disregards the rules of the WTO, and attempt to reform rules according to Chinese standards and practices.

This includes tariffs on imported products from Europe and America and a disregard for internationally accepted trade legislation and rules. Massive subsidies are paid to beneficiary companies, intellectual property theft occurs, technology is transferred illegally and trading practises in most situations only benefit China. Companies under the control of the CCP sell goods and services at a lower price to gain market access.

The quest to build military bases overseas is imperialistic and out of step with military developments in the rest of the world. In Africa, the planned construction of more bases is against the will and wishes of Africans and an attempt to expand military power. The building of these bases will put African countries under direct military control of the CCP. In the economic field, the CCP already occupies leadership positions in various international organizations to the advantage of China. The goal is to establish a Chinese-centered international order. The CCP shows little respect for human rights by restricting the freedom of Chinese citizens, enforcing population control, detaining political opponents without trial, censoring the media and internet, introducing forced labor and restricting religious freedom.

Notes

---

[1] Filesi, Teobaldo. 1972. *China and Africa in the Middle Ages.* Cambridge: Cambridge University Press.

[2] Deng Xiaoping was President of China from 1978 to 1989.

[3] Mao Zedong proclaimed the PRC in 1949 and was president until his death in 1976. Mao's theories, military strategies and political policies determined the direction China took after 1949. Mao recounted his theory of Marxism -Leninism which in collective terms is known as Maoism.

[4] Taylor, Ian. 2018. Mao Zedong's China and Africa. *Twentieth Century Communism* , 15: 47-72.

[5] Gillespie, Sandra. 2004. Diplomacy on a South-South Dimension. In Slavik, Hannah (ed). *Intercultural Communication and Diplomacy*. Geneva: Diplo Foundation: 123.

[6] nytimes.com.1974. Excerpts From Chinese Address to UN Session on Raw Materials. https://www.nytimes.com/1974/04/12/archives/excerpts-from-chinese-address-to-un-session-on-raw-materials.html

[7] Gillespie, Sandra. 2004. Diplomacy on a South-South Dimension. In Slavik, Hannah (ed). *Intercultural Communication and Diplomacy* . Geneva: Diplo Foundation: 123.

[8] digitalarchive.wilsoncenter.org.2020. The Chinese Government's Eight Principles for Economic Aid and Technical Assistance to Other Countries. https://digitalarchive.wilsoncenter.org/document/121560.pdf?v=7842ff83b1fa6e84a7b0e483012dfe15

[9] china.org.cn.2002. Chinese Leaders on Sino-African Relations. http://www.china.org.cn/english/features/China-Africa/82054.htm

[10] Jiang Zemin was the leader of China from 1993 to 2003.

[11] china.org.cn.2002. Chinese Leaders on Sino-African Relations. http://www.china.org.cn/english/features/China-Africa/82054.htm

[12] The One China Policy states that there is only one sovereign Chinese state and that Taiwan is part of this state. This is contrary to the idea that the PRC (China) and the Republic of China (Taiwan) are two separate states.

[13] fmprc.gov.cn.2020. Two Decades of A Shared Journey toward New Heights in the New Era. 16 October. https://www.fmprc.gov.cn/mfa_eng/wjb_663304/wjbz_663308/2461_663310/t1824471.shtml

[14] The ANC has been the ruling party in South Africa since 1994. The PAC is a political party in South Africa that has previously participated in the freedom struggle.

[15] Taylor, Ian. 2006. *China and Africa: Engagement and Compromise* . London: Routledge.

[16] The non-aligned group of countries is a forum of 120 developing countries that does not formally belong to or oppose any major world alliance or grouping. It is the largest political and economic grouping of countries in the world next to the UN.

[17] Servant, Jean-Christophe. 2005. China's trade safari in Africa. http://mondediplo.com/2005/05/11chinafrica

[18] The Chinese Cultural Revolution, formally known as the Great Proletarian Cultural Revolution, was a socio-political movement in China from 1966 until the death of Mao Zedong in 1976. The revolution was a process of purifying Chinese communism of capitalist and Chinese traditions and to unite it under the thinking of Mao. Maoism to this day is the dominant ideology in the CCP. (See MacFarquhar, Roderick and Michael and Schoenhals. 2008. *Mao's Last Revolution*. London: Belknap Press).

[19] The 1911 revolution is also known as the Xinhai Revolution which led to the end of China's last imperial royal house (The Mandarin royal house of Emperor Qing). The founding of the Chinese National Party and the Republic of China was part of the revolutionary process. In Mandarin, the party is known as the Guomintang which in English translates to the National Country Party. (Taiwan is known as the Republic of China or ROC). The first leader of the ROC was Sun Yat-sen who ruled for a short time in 2012. The end of the revolution was marked by uprising and protests against the national government that eventually led to the takeover of China by the communist forces of Mao Zedong. (see Lam, Willy-Lo Lap. 2018. *The Routledge Handbook of the Communist Party of China.* London: Routledge).

[20] The CCP's Great Social and Economic Campaign 'Great Leap Forward' lasted from 1958 to 1962. It is also known as the CCP's second 5-year plan. Mao launched the campaign to transform China from an agricultural to a communist society. The means to achieve this was through the establishment of a communal system. Farmers would supply crops to the commune for joint use. The campaign failed to increase production and an estimated 15-55 million peasants died from hunger. This is considered the largest famine in human history. (see Brown, Kerry. *Hu Jintao : China's Silent Ruler.* California: World Scientific Publishing Company).
China's first 5-year plan, 1953-1957 was a campaign to promote economic growth and industrialization. The steel, coal and heavy machinery industries experienced unprecedented growth during this period. A socialist economic order was also proclaimed during this period. Russia sent experts to provide Mao with advice. (see Taylor, Ian. 2018. Mao Zedong's China and Africa. *Twentieth Century Communism*, 15: 47-72).

[21] Brown, Kerry. 2012. *Hu Jintao : China's Silent Ruler*. UK: Chatham House.

[22] The Soviet Union was a socialist state that included multiple republics of Eurasia. The union existed from 1922 to 1991. The government and economy was centralized with the Communist Party of Russia in control of all the republics. (see Serhii Plokhy. 2015. *The Last Empire: The Final Days of the Soviet Union.* New York: Basic Books).

[23] Shambaugh, David. 2008. *China's Communist Party: Atrophy and Adaptation.* California: University of California Press.

[24] Vogel, Ezra. 2021. The Leadership of Xi Jinping: A Dengist Perspective. *Journal of Contemporary China*, 30 (131): 693-696.

[25] Shambaugh, 2008. *China's Communist Party: Atrophy and Adaptation.*

[26] Ash, Robert. 2007. Quarterly Chronicle and Documentation. *The China Quarterly,* 189: 232–286.

[27] Nathan, Andrew J. and Andrew Scobell. 2012. *China's Search for Security*. New York: Columbia University Press.

[28] Gopal, S. 1989. *Jawaharlal Nehru: A Biography*. Harvard: Harvard University Press.

[29] Arpi, C. 2015. The Panchsheel Agreement. http://www.indiandefencereview.com/spotlights/the-panchsheel-agreement/

[30] Panda, Ankit. 2014. Reflecting on China's Five Principles, 60 Years Later, what are China's 'five principles' worth? 26 June. https://thediplomat.com/2014/06/reflecting-on-chinas-five-principles-60-years-later/

[31] in.china-embassy.org.2004. Build a new international order on the basis of the Five Principles of Peaceful Coexistence. http://in.china-embassy.org/eng/ssygd/fiveprinciple/t82103.htm

[32] tr.china-embassy.org. 2004. Carrying Forward the Five Principles of Peaceful Coexistence in the Promotion of Peace and Development. http://tr.china-embassy.org/eng/xwdt/t140777.htm

[33] timesnownews.com.2017. President Xi Jinping referred to Panchsheel Treaty in meet with PM Modi. Here are the 5 principles mentioned in treaty. 5 September. https://www.timesnownews.com/india/article/GPIcs-china-india-narendra-modi-xi-jinping-panchsheel-treaty/85465

[34] Panda, Ankit. 2014. Reflecting on China's Five Principles, 60 Years Later, what are China's 'five principles' worth? 26 June.

[35] Wood, M. 2020. *The Story of China: The Epic History of a World Power from the Middle Kingdom to Mao and the China Dream.* New York: St. Martin's Press.

[36] Richardson, S. 2009. *China, Cambodia, and the Five Principles of Peaceful Coexistence.* Columbia: Columbia University Press.

[37] Nathan, Andrew J. and Andrew Scobell. 2012. *China's Search for Security.*
[38] Chan, Phil CW 2015. *China, State Sovereignty and International Legal Order.* Leiden: Brill Nijhoff.
[39] Nathan, Andrew J. and Andrew Scobell. 2012. *China's Search for Security.*
[40] The General Secretary of the Central Committee of the CCP is the leader of China, the head of the CCP, the highest official in government, a standing member of the Politburo and head of the secretariat. The Central Committee of the CCP is a political body composed of the top members of the CCP. The committee currently has 205 permanent and 171 rotating members. The Politburo is the decision-making body of the CCP. The bureau currently has 25 members. Both current members of the Central Committee and Politburo were elected during the 19th National Party Congress in 2017. The Secretariat is responsible for the administrative functions of the Politburo on a day-to-day basis. (see Lam, Willy-Lo Lap. 2018. *The Routledge Handbook of the Communist Party of China* . London: Routledge).
[41] Bougon, Francois. 2018. *Inside the Mind of Xi Jinping* . London: C Hurst & Co Publishers Ltd.
[42] Martin, Peter. 2021. *China's Civilian Army: The Making of Wolf Warrior Diplomacy.* Oxford. Oxford University Press.
[43] Smith, Stephen N. 2021. China's 'Major Country Diplomacy': Legitimation and Foreign Policy Change. *Foreign Policy Analysis*, 17 (2): 78-90.
[44] Ogden, Chris. 2019. *A Dictionary of Politics and International Relations in China*. Oxford: Oxford University Press.
[45] Lau, Victor. 2017. *Xi Jinping's Basic Policy on Socialism with Chinese Characteristics for the New Era: Visual Guide to Chinese Communist Party's game plan Announced at 19th National Congress* . California: CreateSpace Independent Publishing Platform.
[46] Ross, Terrill. 2000. *Mao: A Biography: Revised and Expanded Edition.* Stanford: Stanford University Press.
[47] Seek truths from facts 'seek truth from facts' is a historical Chinese expression dating to the era of the Han princely house (202 BC to 220 AD). It originally referred to an approach to study and research. Mao used the term at the 6th National Congress of the CCP in 1938 to refer to innovation and development as drivers of economic growth. In the modern context it is known as research and development. Deng Xiaoping used the term to encourage economic and political reforms. (see Shambaugh, 2008. China's Communist Party: Atrophy and Adaptation).
[48] Baum, Richard. 1996. *Burying Mao: Chinese politics in the age of Deng Xiaoping* . Princeton: Princeton University Press.

[49] Brown, Kerry. 2012. Hu Jintao : China's Silent Ruler. California: World Scientific Publishing Company.
[50] Yang, Jiemian. 2013. China's Diplomacy: Theory and Practice. New Jersey: World Century Publishing Corporation.
[51] Wang, Yizhou. 2018. Creative Involvement: The Transition of China's Diplomacy. London: Routledge.
[52] fmprc.gov.cn.2019. Building on 70 Years of Achievements and Pursuing Progress in the New Era. 24 December. https://www.fmprc.gov.cn/mfa_eng/wjdt_665385/zyjh_66539 1/t1727381.shtml
[53] Veg, Sebastian. 2014. China's Political Spectrum under Xi Jinping. 11 August. https://thediplomat.com/2014/08/chinas-political-spectrum-under-xi-jinping/

Chapter 3 : National and International Security

Background Overview

A military base in Djibouti , increasing participation in UN peacekeeping missions, benevolent visits by naval vessels to international ports and joint operations with Russia in the Mediterranean and Baltic seas. These activities all point to the Chinese People's Liberation Military(PLA) ambitions to play a greater role in international security.[1] While it is true that Chinese troops have been involved in a number of operations outside the Asia-Pacific region, including anti-piracy operations since 2008 in the Gulf of Aden and contributions to peacekeeping missions since the early 1990s, China's military strategy has recently gained momentum under the tenure of Xi Jinping.

This change in strategy is clearly reflected in the Department of Defense's White Paper of 2015 , which spells out a new set of strategic objectives for the military. The projection of military power into the international arena to protect overseas interests and citizens is one of the main objectives. The strategic change in policy underscores the increased, international focus of the military's new historic operations. These are operations away from home in a series of new scenarios and situations. Xi Jinping's goal of increasing the PLA's international status took shape during the 19th National Congress of the CCP in October 2017. Xi stated that the PLA needs to be transformed into a world-class military that can execute the party's policies, that can win wars and that can maintain international, professional standards.[2]

There are several drivers behind the new perspective and strategy. First, the shift in priorities is an indication of changes that are taking place in China's local political and economic environment, which are then projected to the international environment. Since the takeover of Xi, China has shown more open and assertive behavior in the international arena. Xi even set a deadline for the process. By 2049, China must be a modern, strong, culturally educated and harmonious society. At the same time, China must be able to protect its international interests from terrorist attacks, public unrest, anti-Chinese sentiments, as well as local expectations that Beijing will act to protect the interests of citizens. Security needs to be sharpened especially in countries where Chinese citizens work, for example on BRI routes.

Despite changes in policy and the mandate of the military to play a greater international security role, the international outreach of the PLA remains limited. One major shortcoming is operational experience in a real war situation. America and its allies' participation in wars in the Middle East and Afghanistan gives them an advantage over China in terms of operational experience. In each of the conflict areas, Beijing refused to get involved due to the principles of non-interference and non-use of aggression. The PLA's participation in international military activities is limited to military operations other than war (MOOTW).[3]

The PLA has launched a large-scale campaign to modernize the military. One of the steps includes the demobilization of 300,000 soldiers and the replacement of former military regions with operational command structures. The Central Military Commission's (SMC's) four former departments are divided into 15 smaller units that report directly to the SMC. Two new military divisions were also established: the artillery corps' missile force and the strategic support force. On the other hand, China's military budget doubled to 1.1 trillion USD between 2010 and 2020. Naturally, financial support is important to modernize any military in the world and this includes the PLA. China's quest to build a world-class military is beginning to take shape. The PLA's participation in international, multilateral operations offers Chinese troops the opportunity to gain experience and the sharing of knowledge. Despite more assertive and extensive actions in areas away from home, China still follows the Five Principles of Peaceful Coexistence.[4]

The 2015 anti-terrorism bill provides a legal framework for Chinese troops to conduct international anti-terrorism operations. This is the first time that such a bill has been approved by the CCP. However, the Department of Defense's White Paper makes it clear that China will not engage in unilateral military operations away from home. An exception to this rule is military intervention in the South China Sea and Taiwan. These areas are viewed as Chinese territory, falling under the jurisdiction of China. China will continue to invest in the modernization of the military and troops will be deployed in overseas missions. Furthermore, the new strategy will help build China's international status and establish a Chinese-centered, world order.

After the end of the Cold War and the beginning of the 21st century, China formulated a new security concept that laid down the foundations for the maintenance and expansion of international security. The aim of the new security concept was to replace the traditional principles of military alliances and armaments with principles of development, harmony and peace. The core principles of the new concept are mutual trust and respect, equality and cooperation, shared interests between nations and the pursuit of a common future for all countries in the world. Chinese leaders have argued that the security concept can also strengthen the following actions. First, the implementation of platforms promoting dialogue and trust and second, the pursuit of security through cooperation and common development. The new security concept is based on the Five Principles of Peaceful Coexistence.[5]

The National Strategy of China

China's main strategy at the national level is the revival of nationalism. The goal is achieve this strategy by 2049. The political and social ideas of the people need to be incorporated into national policies and strategies. This will help build national power, create a well-functioning system of government and create a Chinese-centered international order. The CCP outlines the strategy as a revival of nationalism, display of power, prosperity, and international leadership.[6] Economic development is a key driver of China's progress and also a necessary component for the PLA to modernize. China aims to transform the PLA into the largest, national military in the world within the next 5 years.[7]

The revival of Chinese nationalism dates back to the disintegration of the Qing dynasty in the early 19th century. It was a period when Western countries abused the political and economic instability in China for their own benefit. In Chinese history, the 19th century is known as the age of humiliation. With the establishment of the PRC in 1949, nationalism began to grow under the local population and used by leaders from Deng Xiaoping to Hu Jintao to unite the nation. Xi Jinping describes the revival of Chinese nationalism as the CCP's original vision and dream.

The sense of national revival is deeply rooted in China's political identity. The disintegration of political processes, repeated violations of China's sovereignty by other powers, and the absence of political and economic security, were drivers for the pursuit of nationalism.[8] President Jiang Zemin unofficially referred to the concept of socialism with Chinese characteristics during the National People's Congress in the early 1990s, but it was only when Hu Jintao became president that the concept started to gain prominence. Under Xi Jinping the concepts of socialism with Chinese characteristics and the rise of nationalism are used interchangeably. In a speech before the CCP's Central Committee in 2013, Xi referred to the importance of an ideology in overcoming China's historical problems. According to Xi, the leadership of the CCP is fully capable of leading China on the path of progress and prosperity. Any deviation from socialism with Chinese characteristics would plunge the country into chaos and be a setback for the creation of wealth. Xi stated that only socialism can save China and only socialism with Chinese characteristics can develop China.[9]

Leaders in the CCP agree that socialism can yield the best economic and social results for the country. The party is absolutely committed to the principles of socialism, but also believes that China must gradually modernize to keep pace with the rest of the world. Consistent with this view, it is essential that China adheres to the four principles of Deng Xiaoping to become a modern socialist state.

The four principles are; the party must continue to follow the path of socialism, the party must continue to elect the General Secretary who is also the president of the country, the party must continue to elect leaders who advocate socialism, and the party must continue to pursue Marxism-Leninism and the thinking of Mao Zedong as ideological basis. These four principles are the building blocks that hold the party structures together and serve as a guideline for political reforms and foreign policy. At a party congress in 2014, Xi Jinping declared that China should not imitate western forms of government and capitalism to become a modern society. China must determine its own path of prosperity and progress through maintaining stricter party discipline and eradicating corruption.

Xi Jinping's focus on building the party's organizational capacity and promoting internal unity is a prominent feature of his tenure. For example, the agenda of the 5th plenary session of the CCP in October 2020 focused strongly on the improvement of the CCP's government systems throughout Chinese society. A consequence of the plenum was that Xi managed to foster unanimity among party members and a blueprint was finalized that spelled out China's economic and social policy for the period 2021-2025.[10]

During the 6th plenary session held in November 2021, Chinese leaders again emphasized that the development of socialism with Chinese characteristics is the main priority of the CCP. Maintaining President Xi Jinping's position in the Central Committee and promoting cohesion in the party is non-negotiable. Furthermore, it is the duty of party members to promote the Chinese dream of national unity among all sections of the population.[11]

The leadership of the CCP regards strategic rivalry with other powers as one of the country's biggest external threats. From the end of Mao's tenure to the present era, a period of about 70 years, Chinese leaders acknowledge that the ideology of socialism is leading to great tensions with the West. Several Chinese governments have formulated strategies to reduce unnecessary tensions with the West. Xi Jinping stated that different government systems lead to rivalry, but that it also holds great benefits for China. In this regard, he refers to international relations based on two fundamental concepts, namely cooperation and conflict. In line with these concepts and China's goal of taking its rightful place in the world, the CCP needs to be adaptable and patient. In a speech delivered before the CCP's Central Committee in 2013, Xi claimed that Western systems, economically, technologically and militarily are superior to China, but that China can reach the same level through hard work and dedication. The pursuit of socialism compared to capitalism is the ultimate goal. If this goal is achieved, China will win the initiative and occupy the dominant position in the world.

In the years before the dissolution of the Soviet Union, leaders in the CCP already realized that the international order was moving towards a multipolar system. When Deng Xiaoping became president, he initiated new initiatives to place China under a path of development. Despite the fact that China benefits greatly from the current international order, the party considers certain systemic aspects to be incompatible with the country's national strategy. In place of the current international order that focuses on the promotion of democracy and liberal values and norms, China strives for an international community where values and norms are shared by all people.[12]

The People's Liberation Army

China's 2019 defense white paper states that the military should play a more active role in advancing foreign policy. The linking of defense and foreign policy within the framework of major power diplomacy is currently one of the CCP's most important international goals. China views the link as necessary to obtain strategic goals and is confident that the military can perform the task. Furthermore, the military must take an active part in the reform of international security, in particular the protection of Chinese interests. [13]

Military diplomacy contributes to the development of strategic partnerships and the reform of international security. The establishment of new foreign military relations seeks to expand China's international security network. By the end of 2020, the Chinese military has put in place mechanisms for better communication on defense and security with more than 50 countries in the world. Many of the countries are in Africa. However,

China's motivation to promote military diplomacy with other countries depends to a large extent on those countries' willingness to follow the new diplomatic framework.

Large-scale changes are taking place within the international strategic landscape. As international powers find new allies, new markets emerge and developing countries grow, the distribution of strategic power between states is also becoming more balanced. The international community strives for peace, stability and development and is not a hegemonic system characterized by power politics, unilateralism and persistent conflicts and wars. However, strategic competition in the international arena is on the rise. America has adapted its National Security Strategy (NSS), defense policies and diplomatic relations with other countries to address any competition.

For China, this means increased competition in the ability to develop nuclear weapons, the space race and the use of long-range missiles as defense and offensive weapons. Furthermore, there are restrictions on arms control and disarmament with signs of an arms race between China, America, and Russia. The withdrawal of weapons of mass destruction also remains problematic. Terrorism and extremism are spreading at a rapid pace. Non-traditional security threats such as cyber security, biosecurity and piracy present challenges. China's international interests are threatened by instability in countries on BRI routes, tariffs on trade, customs and duties and other economic constraints. Embassies, businesses and citizens staff are also being attacked around the world with loss of human lives and damage to buildings and equipment.[14]

The new comprehensive concept of security links national interests with international interests. One of the goals of the Chinese military is to protect the rights and interests of Chinese citizens living abroad. The same goal also applies to Chinese companies and international institutions. Furthermore, the PLA is actively promoting international security and military cooperation with other countries.

In order to improve the PLA's international mobility, new bases are build, logistical capabilities are sharpened, and new military skills are acquired. The Chinese navy, for example, was trained to protect container-and-oil tankers and sea lines of communications. In the event of natural disasters, such as earthquakes, typhoons and tidal waves, the navy is able to evacuate civilians quickly. And the navy can also enforce and maintain maritime law as set out in the constitution. In August 2017, the Djibouti support base was built. The base provides equipment for soldiers and medical equipment for personnel. The base is also used as a launching area for joint exercises with other countries in the region, such as Eritrea, Sudan and Yemen. In 2015, the security situation in Yemen deteriorated to such an extent that the Chinese navy was called in to bring citizens of other countries to safety. Citizens of Italy, Poland, Germany, England and Japan were rescued.[15]

Chinese foreign policy strongly focuses on cooperation between countries to promote common interests. China is building new relationships with foreign armies that are multidimensional, large in scope and operating at multiple levels. By the end of 2020, China had established military exchange programs with 150 countries, established 130 military offices in other countries, while 116 countries had opened military offices in China. In addition, 54 defense liaison offices were established to promote military dialogue. Since 2012, Chinese high-level military officers have visited more than 60 countries while military chiefs from more than 100 countries have visited China.[16]

China's New Security Paradigm

The Central Military Commission (SMC) is the parallel national defense organization of the CCP and the government. On the one side, the SMC is a body controlled by the Central Committee of the CCP and on the other side, the SMC is a body controlled by the Standing Committee of the National People's Congress.[17] The SMC, which is controlled by the National People's Congress, is the military division of the national government.

The National Army, the National Police Service and the Civilian Force fall under the direct command of the SMC. The SMC is controlled by the Standing Committee of the National People's Congress (NPC). The SMC, which falls under the Standing Committee of the NPC, is the highest military command structure and serves under the chairmanship of the General Secretary. The General Secretary is elected by the National People's Congress. In reality, however, the SMC is still controlled by the CCP's Central Committee.

Both committees have seven members and are actually one identical body with two different names. The reason for the two different names is to fit within the structures of the state and within the structures of the CCP. Xi Jinping is currently the General Secretary of the CCP as well as the leader of the country. The committees are tasked with providing guidance to the recruiting of military personnel, the deployment of troops and the military budget. Almost all the members of the SMC are senior military generals, but the most important posts have always been filled by the CCP's most senior leaders. This is to ensure absolute loyalty of the military to the party. By the end of 2018, the SMC exercised control over 7 million members of the military. The SMC's headquarters is located in the Department of Defense's building in Beijing.[18]

The Central National Security Commission (CNSC) was established during the 3rd plenary session of the 18th Central Committee in November 2013. The CNSC is viewed as a major regrouping of the CCP's top structure. The CNSC seeks to consolidate the security apparatus of all the CKP's main components. This includes the Politburo as one of the most important components of the

CCP's political and security structure. The components are now integrated within a single entity under the direct control of Xi Jinping. The goals of the CNSC include combating terrorism, separatism and religious extremism. In addition, the commission liaises with security agencies from other countries to address issues of joint security and crisis management.[19]

The establishment of the CNSC is one of the most concrete and meaningful outcomes of reforms in China's security apparatus in the laste decade. For more than 10 years, a debate has been held in the top structures of the CCP as to whether China needs a national security council. In its current form, the CNSC gives more executive power to the leader of China and is a main body to develop security goals.[20]

Xi Jinping's Concept of Security

Xi Jinping's approach to national security, both domestic and foreign, is a defining feature of his leadership. The 2008 global financial crisis and America's 2009 Asia rebalancing strategy, were main reasons for the review of China's concept of national security. In 2014, shortly after Xi Jinping took over the leadership of China, the new comprehensive security concept was articulated during a session of the CNSC. During the meeting it was proposed that all the different national policy areas be united under one framework. In a successive step, the Politburo approved the CNSC in January 2015. The CNSC was now tasked with developing a new security strategy for China that could also serve as a security theory with Chinese characteristics.[21]

The initial plan was to develop a security council similar to those of western countries. Security councils in western countries focus mainly on national security as an element of foreign policy. However, in China's view the CNSC would differ from western security councils in the following ways.

First, China's concept of national security focuses more on internal risks and threats. Most of the CNSC meetings focus on internal security issues, for example Xinjiang, Hong Kong, Taiwan and the effects of global pandemic on social stability. The phrase internal disorder leads to external adversity was developed by previous governments to indicate the link between internal and external security. This means that internal disorder is a precursor to an external attack on Chinese policy, sovereignty or security. The Taiwan issue is probably the best example to show this connection. China regards Taiwan as a breakaway province, which is historically part of China. The people of Taiwan are connected to China because of language, culture and demographics and should integrate with China to form one Chinese identity. However, Western democracies and several other countries reject the one-China policy and prefer the one-country-two-systems policy. The rejection of the one-China policy is seen by the CCP as an external attack on the sovereignty and territorial integrity of China.[22]

However, Chinese political experts disagree with Xi Jinping's view that internal, non-traditional security issues pose the greatest threats to China. Previous leaders have focused on external security issues. In the new strategy, external threats are observed and analyzed to the extent that they affect social stability and political security at home. Moreover, internal and external influences are often intertwined and mutually inclusive. This includes legal political and economic instruments of state control and the exercise of power.[23]

The goal at the most basic level is to ensure that Xi Jinping is the paramount leader and exercise control over the CCP.

Xi Jinping declared that political security is the lifeblood of national security. Political security is defined as the protection of the party's leadership, the socialist system and the authority of the Central Committee. The Ministry of State Security gives practical implementation to the concept, as the department is responsible for securing political structures in the country.[24]

Threats are not only detrimental to the maintenance of China's material interests, but also have the potential to break up the ideological structure of the party. The interconnection of party structures around a united and centralized ideological basis is crucial to ensure the survival of the party. Xi Jinping suggested that mechanisms should be implemented for the early detection of ideological threats.

The focus on establishing a strong ideological base dates back to the former Soviet Union's failure to hold the communist party system together. Xi Jinping believes that the fall of communism in the Soviet Union was due to a lack of ideological solidarity, corruption, mismanagement of the population's ethnic groups, and inadequate control over the state machinery. The new security concept is an attempt to strengthen the CCP's ideological base by learning from the failures of the Soviet Union.

The composition of security under the new concept is very detailed. Xi Jinping's original formulation of the new concept includes eleven types of security. These include politics, territory, military, economics, culture, society, science, technology, information, ecology, finance and nuclear physics. Other sources include health services and education. This broad typology means that almost any political, economic and social phenomenon is considered a security threat. By the end of 2020, the concept has been expanded to include a further 16 types with new fields being added regularly. These include the traditional areas of political, territorial and military security, along with new areas of cultural, scientific and foreign security.

The comprehensive national security concept argues that opportunities and threats pave the way for a new era of China's international involvement. The phrase, 'the 100-year-old changes within China of which the world is unaware' points to the connection between opportunities and threats. The phrase includes ideas that make China the center of modern civilization and indicates the great revival of the Chinese nation that is going to take place. Proactive action is the answer to prevent potential threats at all levels of government. Furthermore, senior leaders in the CCP believe that conflicting arguments and destabilizing behavior should be eliminated. The goals is to move away from statements that refer to maintaining stability to more aggressive and assertive behavior. Among other things, a new national information system has been set up where members of the public can report negative attitudes and apostate behavior towards the government.[25]

In order to ensure the survival of the CCP, Xi Jinping undertook to keep Western ideas and influences out of China. Examples of this are seen in the closure of Western media offices in China and the restriction placed on the teaching of foreign languages in China (the learning of foreign languages such as English and French are totally banned in some areas). However, schools offering Russian as a foreign language have no restrictions. Russia is one of China's strongest allies and the relationship with President Vladimir Putin forms the basis of a strong Asia-Pacific security network.[26]

The preservation of system stability and survival of the CCP has always been the top priority of Chinese leaders. National security is the brick that anchors the various pillars of government. With the establishment of the PRC, the focus was exclusively on traditional security issues. The protection of Chinese territorial integrity against aggression by America and the Soviet Union and the maintenance of independence were key objectives. This was the situation until the end of Deng Xiaoping's term in the late 1980s. With Jiang Zemin's takeover as General Secretary of the CCP in 1989, chances of engaging in a war with America diminished.

It is in this period that non-traditional elements of security became part of the national security agenda. As China opened up to the rest of the world, other international security issues became prominent. These include economic growth, industrialization, transnational crime, and ideological solidarity with partners in Africa, Asia and South America. New instruments were needed to ensure the security and survival of the CCP.

It was a period when China's development goals took center stage in party meetings. Deng Xiaoping's reform and going out policies signaled this new development phase. The focus was now on economic growth and long-term stability to the country. But to grow economically, China had to enter into cooperation agreements with the west. This led to the joining of various international organizations, such as, the World Health Organization (WHO) and the World Trade Organization (WHO). Diplomacy was also used to discuss and negotiate international issues with leaders from other countries, such as human rights and climate change. It is however true that forms of diplomacy used by previous leaders are irrelevant in the current political climate. The focus in the era of Xi Jinping is to provide assistance to China's international partners in order to create a peaceful and secure climate for the promotion of trade and the protection of mutual interests.[27]

The International Environment: External Threats to Local Stability

The CCP is aware of external threats to domestic stability. The link between domestic and international security issues is crucial to lay a solid foundation for national security. The new, expanded profile includes all policy areas and role players, domestic and international, that could have a potential impact on China's development. From trade relations with other countries to China's international prestige and status; everything now falls under the category of national security. Developments in the domestic environment underscore the importance of a sound national security policy. The policy is also influenced by the international environment. Global pandemics is an example of a security challenge facing China internationally.[28]

The passive defense of China's national security under the new model is not enough. The CCP has therefore decided to take a proactive approach by incorporating external threats within the framework of the new security policy. This will make the future of the party safer in the long run. Xi Jinping stated that the party desires to establish a new set of rules for international relations and to unite humanity under common and shared interests. One of the elements includes an international security community. This community will play a central role in reforming the global order according to China's perspective. The security community will help China exercise control over the international environment and thus prevent threats from liberal Western democracies.

Although mechanisms for local environmental control have been implemented by the CCP, many external challenges remain. The 14th 5-year plan of 2021 states that the scientific and technological revolution, trade shortcomings and the international shift of power are some of the biggest problems facing China.[29] The plan mentions the current trend towards deglobalization, increased tensions with America and attempts to disconnect China from countries that have a preference to trade with Western countries.

The CCP also disapproves of western international models for development and financial management. The decision to follow a Chinese model for international development aims to stop or greatly reduce the dominant influence of America in the world. According to Chinese leaders, American global domination poses a greater danger to the world than the rise of a Chinese-centered world order.[30]

The CCP will attempt to counter threats to the party's survival. The application of Chinese laws abroad will enable the CCP to exercise control over Chinese-based narratives. In this new paradigm, all matters are viewed through the lens of security and the party may take aggressive and coercive actions to protect interests, citizens and the image of China. Examples of the international application of the new security concept include the Hong Kong National Security Act passed by the government in 2020, the risk of loading Huawei into overseas 5G networks and steps taken against Australia to conduct an independent investigation into launching the origins of the Covid-19 pandemic.[31]

These examples are all viewed as threats to China's national security. The Chinese Minister of Justice in 2020 stated that the international application of the laws will increase in intensity. China will fight to improve standards and procedures for enforcing Chinese laws abroad and expanding the international influence of China's legal system.[32]

The Future of the Party

The CCP is confident that success will be achieved on the road ahead. Since Xi Jinping took over the leadership of the CCP, a new approach to national security has been formulated. The new approach aims to ensure the survival of the party and includes all the other elements of policy formulation. A solid institutional and constitutional framework has been created to implement the new approach. Although China's foreign policy principles remain unchanged, the CCP has reformulated a wide range of economic, cultural, military and diplomatic policy objectives. The new paradigm has brought about a definite change in China's international behavior.

China's broad definition of national security gives rise to a wider list of issues that the CCP views as an attack on the country's national interests. This has an immediate effect on trading partners and competitors. Other countries must now be prepared to negotiate with an aggressive and powerful China. The chance of an escalation of conflict is not excluded in this tense situation. The imposition of sanctions against several European countries that do not want to accept quotas on tariffs and other trade restrictions is an example of the aggressive action.

However, the situation in Africa is different. African countries' political and economic bargaining power is weak in manipulating the terms and conditions of trade relations with China. The outcomes are usually negotiated in China's favor without the need for sanctions. The CCP's increased focus on enforcing Chinese legislation and narratives outside China's borders will also affect relations with other countries, both in the public and private sectors. It is highly likely that foreign companies will have to choose between the CCP's policies and the values and interests of their own countries. Xi Jinping on more than one occasion in the last 5 years stated that diplomats should create a favorable foreign environment that can allow China to achieve its development goals.

Notes

[1] Ding, Arthur S. and Jagannath P. Panda. 2021. Chinese Politics and Foreign Policy under Xi Jinping. The Future Political Trajectory. London: Routledge: 9.
[2] Cordesman, Anthony. H and Grace Hwang. 2021. Updated Report: Chinese Strategy and Military Forces in 2021. 3 August. https://www.csis.org/analysis/updated-report-chinese-strategy-and-miitary-forces-2021
[3] Bitzinger, Richard A and James Char. 2019. Reshaping the Chinese Military: The PLA's Roles and Missions in the Xi Jinping Era. London: Routledge: 21.
[4] Mikko., Lee, John and Helena Legarda. 2021. The CCP's next century: expanding economic control, digital governance and national security. June 15. https://merics.org/en/report/ccps-next-century-expanding-economic-control-digital-governance-and-national-security
[5] fmprc.gov.cn. 2021. China's Position Paper on the New Security Concept. https://www.fmprc.gov.cn/ce/ceun/eng/xw/t27742.htm
[6] Cordesman, Anthony. H and Grace Hwang. 2021. Updated Report: Chinese Strategy and Military Forces in 2021.
[7] Ding, Arthur S. and Jagannath P. Panda. 2021. Chinese Politics and Foreign Policy under Xi Jinping: 30.
[8] Xi, Jinping. 2014. The Chinese Dream of the Great Rejuvenation of the Chinese Nation. Beijing. Foreign Language Press.
[9] Boer, Roland. 2021. Socialism with Chinese Characteristics . New York. Springer.
[10] Tiezzi, Shannon. 2020. China's Fifth Plenum: What You Need to Know. 29 October. https://thediplomat.com/2020/10/chinas-fifth-plenum-what-you-need-to-know-2/
[11] Turland, Jesse. 2021. China's Sixth Plenum Report Proclaims Bright Future Under Xi https://thediplomat.com/2021/11/chinas-sixth-plenum-report-proclaims-bright-future-under-xi/
[12] Xiao, Ren and Liu, Ming. 2020. Xi Jinping's Vision of a Community with a Shared Future for Humankind A Revised International Order? Washington: The National Bureau of Asian Research Publishers: 3-10.
[13] Cordesman and Hwang. 2021. Updated Report: Chinese Strategy and Military Forces in 2021.
[14] Wuthnow, Joel., Ding, Arthur S., Saunders, Phillip C., Scobell, Andrew and Andrew ND Yang. 2021. The PLA Beyond Borders: Chinese Military Operations in Regional and Global Context. Washington, DC: National Defense University Press.

15 Greitens, Sheena, C. 2019. Domestic Security in China under Xi Jinping. China Leadership Monitor, 59: 1-19.
16 Wuthnow, Ding, Saunders, Scobell and Yang. 2021. The PLA Beyond Borders: Chinese Military Operations in Regional and Global Context .
17 The National People's Congress (NPC) is the highest body of state power and legislature in China. The Standing Committee is the permanent body of the NPC responsible for decision-making and drafting legislation.
18 Bitzinger and Char. 2019. Reshaping the Chinese Military: The PLA's Roles and Missions in the Xi Jinping Era: 22.
19 Wuthnow, J. 2017. China's New 'Black Box': Problems and Prospects for the Central National Security Commission. The China Quarterly: 887-890.
20 Grünberg, Nis., Drinhausen, Katja., Huotari, Hu, Weixing. 2016. Xi Jinping's Big Power Diplomacy and China's Central National Security Commission (CNSC). Journal of Contemporary China, 25 (98): 163–177.
21 Ding and Panda. 2021. Chinese Politics and Foreign Policy under Xi Jinping. The Future Political Trajectory: 15.
22 Greitens, Sheena, C. 2021. The United States' Strategic Competition with China. 8 June. https://www.armed-services.senate.gov/imo/media/doc/06.08%20Greitens%20Testimony.pdf
23 Greitens, Sheena C. 2020. Dealing with Demand for China's Global Surveillance Exports. April. https://www.brookings.edu/research/dealing-with-demand-for-chinas- global-surveillance-exports /
24 Greitens, 2021. The United States' Strategic Competition with China.
25 Greitens, 2019. Domestic Security in China under Xi Jinping. China Leadership Monitor: 5-10.
26 Grünberg, Drinhausen, Huotari and Hu. 2016. Xi Jinping's Big Power Diplomacy and China's Central National Security Commission (CNSC): 163–177.
27 Greitens, 2019. Domestic Security in China under Xi Jinping. China Leadership Monitor: 5-10.
28 Ding and Panda. 2021. Chinese Politics and Foreign Policy under Xi Jinping. The Future Political Trajectory: 25-30.
29 The 14th 5-year plan for the period 2021 to 2025 covers all the economic, social and environmental aspects of development. The plan was officially ratified by the National People's Congress on March 11, 2021. (See Tiezzi, 2020. China's Fifth Plenum: What You Need to Know. October 29. Https://thediplomat.com/2020/10/chinas-fifth-plenum -what-you-need-to-know-2 /)
30 Xiao and Liu. 2020. Xi Jinping's Vision of a Community with a Shared Future for Humankind A Revised International Order?
31 The Hong Kong National Security Act of 2020 stipulates that the city is under Chinese control and that cession, terrorism 85

and foreign interference in the city's administration are prosecuted.
[32] Turland, 2021. China's Sixth Plenum Report Proclaims Bright Future Under Xi.

Chapter 4 : Security in Africa: Strategy and Policy

Historical Overview

China's historical ties with Africa date back to the 1950s, a year after the PRC was established. The government of Mao Ze Dong decided at an early stage to support African countries' struggle for independence. However, it was only during the Bandung Conference in 1955 that a foundation for China-Africa solidarity was established. During this conference, freedom fighters from Africa were housed at the Nanjing Military Academy for training in guerrilla and insurgency warfare. By the end of 1958, more than 3,000 freedom fighters had been trained from Africa, more than 400 requests had been received from freedom groups for the provision of weapons, and hundreds of Chinese military instructors had been deployed to Africa for the training of freedom fighters.[1]

Between 1958 and 1961, China participated in the Pan-African Congresses in Tunisia and Egypt. These congresses were held to accelerate Africa's goals to decolonization. China supplied large quantities of weapons to freedom groups in Angola, Mozambique and Tanzania, during this time. In comparison to the Soviet

Union and Cuba, China only had a small number of troops. Cuba deployed 370,000 troops in Africa by the end of the 1980s and China about 20,000.[2] The troops were not trained for contact situations. The main task of the PLA was to promote the communist ideology and help build infrastructure. The construction of the 1,860km Tanzania-Zambia railway (TAZARA) was China's largest and most important project in Africa at that time. The construction of the railway was part of the Organization of Africa Unity's (OAU) strategy to make frontline states less dependent on the economy and transport infrastructure of apartheid South Africa and Rhodesia.

The two countries were under the control of minority governments. The frontline states provided bases for training and insurgency to all of Southern Africa's freedom groups. The unstable situations in frontline states presented China with the opportunity to build stronger diplomatic relations. Tanzania's Prime Minister and Secretary-General of the OAU at the time, Salim Ahmed Salim, argued that the construction of the railway showed that China was willing to help African countries. As a gesture of solidarity, African countries voted in 1971 for China to take back its place in the UN General Assembly in the place of Taiwan.[3]

The situation has not changed much since the early years of contact and construction of the TAZARA railway. Although China has fewer troops deployed on the continent than America and France, ideology, politics, and economics are still used to promote closer cooperation. However, calls are on the rise for greater military presence in Africa, as contained in White Papers of Defense from 1995 to 2019.[4]

China's military relations with African countries were divided into six main periods. The first period (1949-1950s) was the beginning of China's military diplomacy in Africa. After the establishment of the PRC in 1949, China reached out to African countries that followed the communist ideology. This has made China a natural partner with these African countries. China also provided military assistance to Muslim countries, for example, Algeria and Egypt.[5]

A major feature of the second period (1960s to early 1970s) was the supply of weapons and ammunition to independent states and liberation movements. While Sino-American relations remained stable during the period, there was a dramatic decline in relations with the Union of Soviet Socialist Republics (USSR) by the end of 1950. During the same period, there was an increase in freedom movements in Africa and Asia. China's focus was on promoting military diplomacy with new independent states. During Prime Minister Zhou Enlai's visit to Africa in 1964, eight principles for providing economic and technological assistance to foreign countries were introduced. These principles also served as a guideline for military aid. Algeria, Egypt, Ghana and Tanzania received weapons and training from China at the time. By the end of 1970, China had sent 1,500 military experts to 25 African countries and trained nearly 5,000 military personnel.

During the third period (from the beginning of 1970 to 1978), relations between China and America were on good footing. China's relations with other countries in the western hemisphere also improved. The goal of China's foreign policy during this period was to stop or equalize the dominance of Soviet military aid to African countries. After construction began on TAZARA, China increased military aid to Tanzania. By the end of 1978, China had trained more than 7,500 military personnel from various African countries.

The fourth period (1979 to 1989) was marked by changes in China's foreign policy. Most African countries gained independence during this period and were developing their economies. Free aid and assistance were discontinued and replaced by a system where military equipment was obtained through loans. As a result of these stricter methods of obtaining weapons, there was a decrease in military aid to liberation movements.

The fifth period (1990 to 1999) started after the end of the Cold War. Military diplomacy with Western countries was at a low point due to a change in the international balance of power and the rise of renewed American power. This shift in power meant new opportunities for military development in China. Since 1993, China's military diplomacy has evolved from a one-dimensional focus on territorial security to a multidimensional focus of greater international display of power. In Africa, the focus shifted to participation in peacekeeping missions and high-level visits by military officials.

The sixth period (2000 to present) shows the greatest development of China's military diplomacy. In 2000,

FOCAC was established, pursuing security cooperation as one of its objectives. The Chinese government declared the security of facilities and citizens working in the BRI a top priority. Various forums and dialogues have also been held over the last decade to promote security cooperation with African countries.[6]

The Goals of Military Diplomacy

China's military diplomacy is important in the context of the country's overall diplomacy and a key instrument to achieve national defense objectives. The nature and extent of military diplomacy in Africa is defined by the country's Africa Policy and National Defense Policy. The security aspects of China's 2015 Africa policy are summarized in the following points. 1) The promotion of peace and security in Africa. China supports African countries' efforts to resolve their local issues themselves. The principles of non-interference, mutual trust and respect for territorial sovereignty form the basis for foreign relations. This includes African countries. However, the Chinese government will do everything in its power to assist African governments in resolving pressing issues. This happens at the request of the governments themselves. Africa is a continent faced by many security issues and it is in this area that China can offer its experience and expertise. China faces similar security issues back home and can share its experience with African countries. In order to improve the business and strategic landscape in Africa, the Chinese government plays a constructive role in promoting peace and security. The Special Representative of the Chinese government in charge of African affairs is tasked to make the relationship run according to plan.

China will continue to promote dialogue and consultation in the areas of security. This happens through the principles of peace through development and development through peace. The implementation of security frameworks based on cooperation and sustainability is one of the main objectives. China will support efforts by the AU and regional organizations to build capacity for peace and security development. The China-Africa Partnership for Peace and Security, Support for the AU's Standing Force and Capacity for Immediate Response to Crises are all part of the framework.

2) The deepening of military cooperation. China will continue to promote military visits and cooperation with

African countries. Of particular importance is the exchange of military knowledge and training to members of African Military. The training of military personnel is a priority and is carried out according to the needs of local armies. Building capacity for the protection of borders, the control of immigrants and refugees, the fight against terrorism and attacks by radical Muslim groups all contribute to security and peace.

3) Supporting African countries in combating non-traditional security threats. China supports African governments in sharing intelligence, knowledge and building capacity to combat non-traditional security threats. These include participation in anti-piracy operations, maritime security in the Gulf of Aden, the coast of Somalia and the Gulf of Guinea. China is ready to promote cooperation between police departments and courts. Both Chinese and Africans can learn from each other's legal systems, especially in areas where differences exist regarding immigration, labor law, business law and customs.

China stands up for the rights and interests of its citizens in Africa and will put in place the necessary measures to protect them. This also applies to Africans who are abused and illegally treated by Chinese employers. China will work with African governments to extradite criminals and send them back to their countries of origin, if convicted as criminal.[7]

The Strategic Importance of Africa

The role of the military significantly changed after the proclamation of an independent foreign policy of peace and development. The military is not only the protector of the country's borders, but helps to initiate and facilitate security cooperation between countries. The military therefore plays a vital, supportive role in implementing the government's foreign policy. The military maintains the Five Principles of Peaceful Coexistence and develops non-allied, non-hostile and non-partisan relations with other countries. The Military seeks to promote communication in maritime security, participates in UN peacekeeping operations, combat terrorism and insurgency and donates funds for natural disaster management.[8]

Against this background, China's military objectives are classified as follows. The first objective is to create a favorable regional and international environment for peaceful development. The rapid growth of China, especially the modernization of the military, is a cause for concern among Western countries as well as countries in the region. African countries in general have high expectations of China and the so-called China Threat Theory creates a position of mistrust for cooperation and economic development. Military diplomacy can eliminate suspicion and promote mutual trust, as already observed in peacekeeping operations, the increase in arms sales and the presence of security contractors.

The second goal is to establish strong bilateral political and economic relations, thus protecting China's national interests on the continent. Military cooperation is an indicator of strong bilateral relations and helps to promote political, economic and security interests. The reciprocal visits of high-level military personnel could further advance cooperation. Non-traditional threats such as terrorism and piracy in Africa still occur, as well as attacks on businesses, investments, civilians and ships.

The training of military personnel provides African countries with the necessary knowledge to resolve local security issues themselves. China's policy of non-interference prevents the military from engaging in political and security situations of diplomatic partners. The third objective focuses on taking on greater international responsibility to promote peace and stability in the world. This is a major goal and extends over the long term. China has a responsibility as a permanent member of the UN Security Council to advance the goal in Africa as well. For this reason, Chinese troops are participating in peacekeeping missions, providing humanitarian assistance in conflict areas and working together to find solutions to non-traditional security issues.[9]

China has been participating in joint military exercises with other countries since the beginning of the 21st century. However, the country's military diplomacy in Africa is not yet on the same level as with Russia and countries in Southeast Asia. Patterns of China's military diplomacy in Africa focus mainly on the following areas: First, military exchanges and communications. It is the most common form of modern military diplomacy and includes visits by high-ranking officials to each other's armies. As highlighted in China's Africa Policy of 2006 and the revised version of 2015, the Chinese military considers military visits to be extremely important in promoting cooperation with African countries. It is an essential component for building trust building and diplomacy. Bilateral military visits between China and Africa for the last decade remain stable at 26 visits per year.[10]

Second, military attachés. By 2018, China had military attachés in 109 countries and 101 countries had opened military offices in China. China appointed 35 military attachés in African countries by the end of 2020, while 41 African countries appointed attachés in China. This is viewed against the background of 54 independent states in Africa and 52 states that have diplomatic relations with China.[11]

Third, defense forums or dialogue. There are several bilateral discussion forums between China and African countries. Of value, however, is the first multilateral defense and security forum which was held in Beijing in June 2018. The forum identified peacekeeping missions and the establishment of peace in post-conflict countries as the main security issues.[12]

Fourth, the visits of warships. In July 2000, a Chinese frigate visited South Africa and Tanzania. This was the Chinese navy's first visit to Africa. In October 2008, a frigate from South Africa visited China. This was the first visit of a South African warship to China. In April 2011, ships from China docked at the port of Durban and in 2012 a Chinese navy visited Alexandria in Egypt.[13]

Fifth, functional exchange visits. High-level visits between members of the Chinese and African Military have increased since the beginning of the 21st century. The purpose of the visits is to share technological knowledge, receive training and create channels for communication. The Chinese hospital ship, the Peace Arc, has been visiting Djibouti, Kenya, Tanzania and the Seychelles since 2010.

For the first time, workshops are also offered to the heads of African military colleges in English, French and Portuguese.

Military assistance. China's military assistance to African countries by the start of the 21st century was still limited. However, it increased with participation in peacekeeping missions. Participation in this UN activity helps to build relationships and determines what resources are needed to advance military diplomacy. China currently provides military knowledge and training to almost all African countries. The main recipients of China's military aid are

Angola, Ghana, Mozambique, Sudan, South Sudan, Tanzania and Zimbabwe. Most of the assistance is in the form of loans or donations of materials and equipment. The loans are used to improve the facilities of receiving countries, such as the construction and repair of headquarters, living quarters, training centers, the upgrading of military communication channels, and the construction of hospitals. The materials and equipment are mostly in the form of uniforms, ambulances, armored vehicles, military trucks and other logistical materials.

Military training. Training is an integral part of China's military diplomacy and focuses on the sharing of knowledge. It includes a wide range of courses, from ideological solidarity with the CCP's military doctrines (Chinese combat techniques and war strategies), logistical support, human resource management, mobility and preparedness, and coastal patrolling (littoral countries).

By the end of 2020, there were more than 30 military training colleges in Africa. Between 4,000 and 6,000 military members from 140 countries received training in China in the last decade. A large number of the personnel came from Africa.[14] The Chinese military medical corps also sends doctors and nurses to African countries to assist with medical services. In Gabon and Liberia, medical clinics are permanently manned by Chinese doctors.[15]

Peace missions in Africa. China feels it is its duty to participate in peacekeeping missions to bring peace and stability to the world. Chinese troops deployed in mission areas are mainly tasked with monitoring ceasefires, maintaining roads, bridges and camp facilities (also from other countries), providing transportation and medical support, community social reconstruction, and humanitarian assistance. By the end of 2019, the Chinese military had participated in 25 peacekeeping missions with other countries. During the period, more than 40,000 soldiers were deployed to the mission areas. China deploys most troops and police members of the UN Security Council's permanent members.

China also sends the most engineers, logistical and medical personnel from the 115 participating countries. In a further step, the financial contribution that China makes is the largest among the developing countries. The majority of China's peacekeeping personnel are now stationed in Africa. [16] Escorting ships to safety. In accordance with UN resolutions, China escorted ships to safety during attacks by pirates in the Gulf of Aden and Somalia in 2008. The operations were primarily aimed at ensuring the safety of Chinese ships and personnel aboard and secondly at ensuring the safe passage of other ships in the region. Escorting ships in these problematic coastal areas is now a regular task of the Chinese navy. China also has a hospital ship called the Peace Ark that provides free medical assistance to Kenya, Tanzania , Djibouti and the Seychelles.[17]

Political party training. The training of political parties and cadres in African socialist countries is another pattern of military diplomacy. The objectives of the programs are to teach political party members socialism with Chinese characteristics, to build party structures similar to those of the CCP, to promote Chinese culture and to develop political leadership. The plan to train political parties are not new, but dates back to 1960s when China supported liberation movements in Africa for independence.

In the modern era, programs have been expanded to provide for work-related-training, such as building organizational structures, creating ideological solidarity, using propaganda techniques and managing party structures.

Furthermore, parties are trained in the Chinese way of government and economic development.[18] Programs are offered across the continent and includes Angola, Ethiopia, Mozambique, Namibia, South Africa, South Sudan, Sudan, Uganda and Zimbabwe. South Africa's ANC sent 4 groups of 56 members for training between 2008 and 2012. In the last few years, programs are developed to train the younger generation in becoming leaders. Between 2011 and 2015, more than 200 young African leaders successfully completed and graduated from the programs. While ruling parties in Africa are enthusiastic about the extent to which the Chinese way of governing can change their party structures, there is also criticism.

The subordination of the military and government departments to the control of the CCP is problematic in the African context. Problematic due to the different systems of government in Africa and the influence that the elite and personality styles of individual leaders have on the party. In Africa, this means that leaders use the military for their own gain and do not take the interests of the community at heart. Recent examples of military dictatorships include Mali, Guineau, Sudan and Chad.

China's growing role as a security player is aimed at protecting its commercial interests and citizens on the continent. Furthermore, it is necessary to sharpen security in order to give legitimacy to the rule of the CCP. China's economic involvement in Africa has grown significantly since the introduction of the going-out-policy in the mid-1990s. One of the objectives of the policy was to give state-owned companies more international exposure.[19]

By the end of 2020, China had funded 18.9% of infrastructure projects in Africa, while 33.2% of the projects had been built by Chinese companies. The presence of Chinese companies is a major reason for the increase in workers to Africa and the rise in security threats. Furthermore, there are hundreds of private companies doing business in more stable African countries. These companies account for nearly 66% of the Gross Domestic Product (GDP) of Sub-Saharan Africa (SSA).

These companies benefit from Africa's low labor costs, which leads to a greater interest among private companies to move production to Africa. Chinese private companies in Africa primarily target local markets rather than to focus on exports. This is beneficial for Africans because jobs are created and technological knowledge is exchanged. The downside is that goods and services are still being sourced from China. In general, countries in Africa have a positive image of the contribution that China makes to promote manufacturing. In the long run, this could lead to greater industrialization. As economic interdependence between Africa and China increases, so does China's definition of national interests. In the last decade, China has begun to step up security on sea routes leading to Africa, especially sea lines of communication. It facilitates and secures the transportation of products and goods between Africa and China.[20]

The China-Africa Cooperation Forum (FOCAC)

FOCAC was established in 2000. In order for African governments to join the Forum, they have to recognize the one-China policy. By the end of 2020, Eswatini was the only country in Africa that still had diplomatic relations with Taiwan. African governments' admission to the

Forum facilitates the institutionalization of regional organizations such as the AU, because the rules, principles and norms are laid out by China and have to be accepted by African governments. The possibility exists that this will amount to the socialization of Africa according to Chinese values and norms.[21]

The Forum has no permanent secretariat; it is organized and coordinated by China's Department of Foreign Relations in Beijing. This department oversees the Forum's agenda, statements and action plans. African governments make only a small contribution to the drafting and functioning of initiatives, but in recent years have created a legal section within the Forum. This section examines the legal aspects of action plans and programs.[22]

Despite China's rhetoric that cooperation is taking place on equal footing, the division of power in the Forum is highly unequal. China is taking advantage of the unequal relationship to expand negotiating power. Furthermore, the forum encourages competition between African countries which is a major challenge for policy coordination between the different countries. This has an impact on governments' diplomatic relations and the formulating of agendas. However, the executive functions of the Forum have changed according to a decision taken by the AU at a meeting in 2017. The decision stipulates that members can only join the meetings when new initiatives and action plans are introduced. This is to limit member's dependency on China's rules, procedures and proposals.[23]

The ideological framework of South-South cooperation is deeply rooted in the structure of the Forum.[24] Documents of the Forum regularly refer to joined setbacks that China and African countries faced in the path to development. The colonial period and imperialism are also cited as factors that hindered progress. This rhetoric emphasizes the common factors of sovereignty, equality and non-interference that gave rise to a new type of strategic partnership between China and Africa.

A key objective of the partnership is to change the international order. The absence of Western political norms and values, such as the protection of human rights and the rule of law in the Forum's agendas, are indicative of this new direction.[25] Documents of the Forum also refer to the concept of African solutions to African problems. This means that African governments should use their own resources to solve local problems. In the context of the Forum, however, the concept has a double meaning for China. On the one hand, China is opposed to the interference of foreign powers in the domestic affairs of African countries. This refers to cases where the common interests of both China and African governments are threatened. Statements and documents in the Forum are compiled to advance the interests of both China and African governments. On the other hand, policies are being drafted to isolate African countries from Western influences so that they can build a preference for the Chinese way of governing.[26]

During early negotiations in the Forum, little attention was paid to security issues. However, those issues became more prominent after China blocked UN action in Darfur. This decision led to fierce criticism from the West and forced China to change its position on non-interference to one of gradual involvement in Africa's peace and security issues.

In 2007, the first Special Representative for African Affairs was appointed. The representative is responsible for holding regular political consultations with African governments on issues of the day. In 2008, the China-

Africa Strategic Security Dialogue and Mechanism was launched; the seventh strategic dialogue was held in 2018. The declaration of the 2012 Forum was strongly inspired by events of the Arab Spring and the removal of the Gaddafi government in 2011. Following the civil war in Libya and the adoption of UN Resolution 1973 (2011), China entered into a partnership with the AU to pursue peace and security on the continent.[27] The 2015 Africa Policy Document expanded on the strategic partnership and stated that China would make financial and logistical contributions to the AU's peace and security architecture. In a further step, greater participation in peace missions was announced.[28]

The AU's Peace and Security Architecture

The AU's Peace and Security Architecture is a protocol adopted by the AU Security Council in July 2002 and implemented in 2003. The protocol aims to prevent, manage and resolve Africa's conflicts and crises. The protocol is built around structures, goals, principles and values as well as decision-making processes. The protocol also applies to post-conflict reconstruction and development. [29] The core of the peace and security architecture are the continental early warning system, the African standing force and the peace fund. Security is also promoted through conflict prevention mechanisms between the AU and various regional organizations. In this regard, the AU's commission for human rights and civil rights plays an important role. The protocol provides for partnerships between the AU and UN on the one hand and other role players. The peace and security framework includes peacemaking, peace support operations, peacebuilding, post-conflict reconstruction and development, the promotion of democratic practices, good governance, human rights and humanitarian aid and disaster management.

The Beijing Platform for Action (2019-2021) serves as the current framework for China's military assistance to Africa. This plan provides for assistance by the military and police in maintaining peace and security. Assistance is also provided for the development of the African Standing Force. The Standing Force is supposed to intervene when human rights are violated, for example, genocide and trafficking in people. Beijing also cooperates with the AU Security Council and regional organizations to bring peace and stability to Somalia and Sudan. In recent developments, equipment was provided for the upgrading of security infrastructure in the Sahel and West Africa.[30]

In the 2000s, China's financial support for peacekeeping operations was relatively low, for example, only 1.8 million USD was spent to the UN mission in Sudan. This is weighed against the total UN budget of 466 million USD allocated to the mission in Sudan in the 2000s. As conflict in Africa began to escalate, larger funds became available. At the FOCAC meeting in 2018, 100 million USD was promised for a period of 3-5 years.[31]

The China-Africa Peace and Security Fund further provides funding in the development of peace and security programs and the establishment of infrastructure. The AU's logistics base in Yaoundé, Cameroon, for example, has been upgraded at a cost of 25 million American dollars. Parts of the fund will also be used for the AU's multinational task force to stop Boko Haram insurgency in Nigeria and for the deployment of police officers for the AU's mission in Somalia.[32]

The total budget for the Peace and Security Fund is 200 million American dollars. This is allocated for a period of three years.[33] The AU and China can strengthen their partnership in the areas of peace and security by exchanging knowledge and developing new skills. The amalgamation of human and natural resources has the potential to further expand the security architecture of Africa.[34]

Since 2015, discussions have been held with representatives of the AU to establish a long-term military presence in Africa. In 2017, China made available 100 million USD for the AU's assistance force and counter-reaction unit. As part of the UN's peacekeeping missions in the DRC, Darfur, Mali, South Sudan and Western Sahara, China will deploy 1,600 personnel and troops by the end of 2025. The creation of a Chinese-centered, Pan-Africanist defense forum is also on the agenda in discussions with the AU. This defense forum will be under direct control of the SMC.[35]

The China-Africa Defense Security Forum

The first China-Africa Defense Security Forum in 2018 highlighted the growing security cooperation between China and Africa. This new platform has brought together representatives from 50 African countries and the AU to discuss multiple military and security issues. The Forum took place at the PLA's University of Defense in Beijing.

African leaders agreed that the Forum should usher in a historic period of China-Africa military relations and develop in the same vein as the established Shanghai Development Corporation (SDC). The SDC is a Eurasian political, economic and security alliance launched on 15 June 2001 in Shanghai, China. The member states are China, Kazakhstan, Kyrgyzstan, Russia, Tajikistan and Uzbekistan.[36] At the first security forum, military issues at top management level was discussed. These included rules, procedures and action plans for future meetings, as well as the developing of programs for the training of African Military. Other goals include creating communication channels between Chinese and African security sectors.

The first Forum was followed by a dialogue in 2019 on security and peace and a second dialogue on law enforcement and security. These dialogues focused on protecting citizens, companies and projects. One of the big points of discussion was the promotion of China's tracking systems to African countries. The tracking systems are particularly useful in combating crime, protecting the public and monitoring the activities of terrorist groups.[37]

The construction of more military bases also received attention. Although not a top priority at this stage, the construction of more military bases has been put on the agenda for future meetings. China currently has one military base in Djibouti and is looking at sites in West and Southern Africa to build more bases. According to Chinese Defense Department officials, Nigeria has offered to make their ports available for use by Chinese naval vessels. The island of Sao Tome and Principe was also approached for the upgrading of an existing port to dock naval vessels.[38]

The American government views China's ambitions to build military bases in Africa and along the coast as a threat. The Pentagon is particularly concerned that a network of military and naval bases will lead to greater strategic competition and an expansion of geopolitical influence.[39] The Pentagon is worried that China will build a base against the Atlantic Ocean that could lead to confrontation with American ships and naval vessels. The sea route from the east coast of America to the west coast of Africa is important for the acquisition of natural resources, such as oil and gas, the provision of equipment for peacekeeping missions and the fight against terrorism and extremism. American cargo ships visits the ports of Lagos and Port Harcourt in Nigeria every month. If China builds a military base on the west coast of Africa, sea lines of communication (SLOCS) between American ships and ports in Africa may be disrupted.[40]

China has enlarged the port of Djibouti to accommodate aircraft carriers and nuclear submarines. The enlarged port is right next to China's Djibouti base. The base was originally developed to provide support in anti-piracy operations off the coast of Somalia. But with piracy declining sharply in the last couple of years, the plan is to use the base as an auxiliary port for naval vessels, such as, the type-075 amphibious assault ship with a helicopter landing pad or the locally-manufactured Type-002 aircraft carrier.

By the end of 2021, China had 2 aircraft carriers and 6 Shang-class nuclear attack submarines (SSNs). Another Shandong Class 3 aircraft carrier is under construction and should be ready for launch in 2024. China also looks at countries further south along the East Coast of Africa to build military bases, targeting Tanzania and Mozambique. These bases will be used not only for stocking up on supplies and refueling, but also to rearm and repairing naval vessels.[41]

The Development of China's Defense Policy and Legal Framework

In the last couple of years there has been a rise in attacks on citizens that lives in war-torn and conflict-ridden countries. This has led to governments changing their defense and security policies to counter these kind of attacks. Recent Chinese defense white papers state that the protection of Chinese property and nationals abroad is a top priority. The term 'Military Operations other than War' (MOOTW) was subsequently adopted from the American defense policy to focus on peacekeeping operations, the evacuation of civilians in war-time, and providing humanitarian aid.

There is also an emphasis on the navy to become an effective, multi-functional naval power in oceans away from home. Furthermore, Article 71 of the 2015 anti-terrorism law allows Chinese security forces to participate in international anti-terrorism operations. According to UN protocol, host countries must give permission to foreign forces to participate in the operations.[42] China's participation in anti-piracy operations in the Horn of Africa in 2008 has also led to more visits by naval vessels to ports in Africa. In 2014, units of the Chinese military conducted joint exercises with the Tanzanian army. In 2018, the navy participated in anti-piracy operations with Gabon, Ghana, Cameroon and Nigeria.[43]

Apart from high-level military visits that regularly take place, training is now an integral part of China's military diplomacy. The aim is to increase the capacity of African armies by teaching the concept of peace through development. In several African countries, however, there are limits to the degree of success achieved due to poor governance and economic growth. These factors do not lead to a reduction of conflict and instability.

In order to achieve positive results, China now focuses on training armies in countries that are more stable and showing signs of economic growth.[44] China's security contractors, for example, are training police officers in Kenya to protect the Mombassa-Nairobi railway line. But in other countries, such as, Uganda, the local military is mainly responsible for protecting Chinese interests and citizens because the population insist.[45]

In several African countries, China has helped with the establishment of military infrastructure. This includes the installation of sensitive information technology networks by Zhongxing Telecommunication Equipment Corporation (ZTE). In Tanzania, China has built a new military training college that includes, among other things, a launch area for amphibious vessels and a tactical combat area for anti-terrorism operations.[46]

The Chinese government also offers military training programs to identify future security leaders and as a platform to promote weapon sales. These military interactions build relationships and is beneficial for the exchange of military knowledge.

Notes

1 Shinn, David H and Joshua Eisenman. 2012. *China and Africa: A Century of Engagement* . Pennsylvania. University of Pennsylvania Press.
2 Castro, Fidel. 2003. *Cold War: Warnings for a Unipolar World.* Melbourne: Ocean Press.
3 Monson, Jamie. 2011. *Africa's Freedom Railway: How a Chinese Development Project Changed Lives and Livelihoods in Tanzania* . Indiana: Indiana University Press.
4 andrewerickson.com.2019. China's Defense White Papers, 1995-2019. https://www.andrewerickson.com/2019/07/china-defense-white-papers-1995-2019-download-complete-set-read-highlights-here/
5 Shen, Zhixiong. 2014. On China's Military Diplomacy in Africa. http://www.siis.org.cn/Research/EnInfo/1702 (accessed 3 December 2021).
6 Xiao, Tianliang. 2011. *Military Diplomacy of PRC* . Beijing: National Defense University Press.
7 chinadaily.com.cn.2015. Full Text: China's second Africa policy paper. 5 December. https://www.chinadaily.com.cn/world/XiattendsParisclimateconference/2015-12/05/content_22632874.htm (accessed 12 December 2021).
8 Devermont, Judd. 2020. China's Strategic Aims in Africa. May 8.https://www.uscc.gov/sites/default/files/Devermont_Testimony.pdf
9 Shen. 2014. On China's Military Diplomacy in Africa.
10 Higgs, Robert. 2021. Naval diplomacy strengthens ties between China and South Africa. 14 June. https://www.iol.co.za/news/politics/opinion/naval-diplomacy-strengthens-ties-between-china-and-south-africa-a351b6ba-45e5-46e1-aa15-861ab1c01119
11 Nantulya, Paul. 2021. China's Blended Approach to Security in Africa. 29 July. https://www.ispionline.it/en/pubblicazione/chinas-blended-approach-security-africa-31216
12 Moynihan, Harriet and Wim Muller. 2019. China's Growing Military Presence Abroad Brings New Challenges. 18 February. https://www.chathamhouse.org/2019/02/chinas-growing-military-presence-abroad-brings-new-challenges
13 Higgs, 2021. Naval diplomacy strengthens ties between China and South Africa.
14 Nantulya, Paul. 2020b. Chinese security contractors in Africa. 8 October. https://carnegietsinghua.org/2020/10/08/chinese-security-contractors-in-africa-pub-82916

[15] reliefweb.int.2021. China Donates Anti-Epidemic Materials to Liberia. https://reliefweb.int/report/liberia/china-donates-anti-epidemic-materials-liberia

[16] Gowan, Richard. 2020. China's pragmatic approach to UN peacekeeping. 14 September. https://www.brookings.edu/articles/chinas-pragmatic-approach-to-un-peacekeeping/

[17] Panda, Ankit. 2018. China Dispatches New Naval Fleet for Gulf of Aden Escort Mission. 11 December. https://thediplomat.com/2018/12/china-dispatches-new-naval-fleet-for-gulf-of-aden-escort-mission/

[18] Herman, Fanie. 2020. China's Party Training Programs in South Africa: A Quest for Political Alignment. Fudan Journal of the Humanities and Social Sciences, 13: 437–451.

[19] Vendryes, Thomas. Chinese firms "going out": An economic dynamic with political significance. China Perspectives, 1: 67-68.

[20] Maru, Mehari T. 2019. Why Africa loves China. 6 June. https://www.aljazeera.com/opinions/2019/1/6/why-africa-loves-china/ (21 September 2021).

[21] Hodzi, Obert. 2018. Delegitimization and 'Re-socialization': China and the Diffusion of Alternative Norms in Africa. International Studies 55 (4) 297–314.

[22] files.ethz.ch.2012. FOCAC Twelve Years Later Achievements, Challenges and the Way Forward. https://www.files.ethz.ch/isn/151831/FULLTEXT01-4.pdf

[23] Kagame, Paul. 2017. Report on the Proposed Recommendations for the Institutional Reform of the African Union. https://au.int/en/documents/20170129/report-proposed-recommendations-institutional-reform-african-union

[24] South-South Cooperation refers to the technical cooperation between developing countries in the southern hemisphere. It is a tool used by states, international organizations, academics, civil society and the private sector to share knowledge, skills and initiatives. Areas of cooperation include health, agriculture, climate change, human rights, migration and urbanization.

[25] Zhao, Suisheng. 2017. China in Africa Strategic Motives and Economic Interests. London: Routledge.

[26] focac.org.2012. The fifth ministerial conference of the forum on China-Africa Cooperation Beijing Action Plan (2013-2015). 23 July. http://www.focac.org/eng/zywx_1/zywj/t954620.htm

[27] zw.china-embassy.org.2012. Open Up New Prospects for A New Type of China-Africa Strategic Partnership. 20 July. http://zw.china-embassy.org/eng/xwdt/t953669.htm

[28] chinadaily.com.cn.2015. Full Text: China's second Africa policy paper. 5 December. https://www.chinadaily.com.cn/world/XiattendsParisclimateconference/2015-12/05/content_22632874.htm

29 peaceau.org.2012. The African Peace and Security Architecture (APSA). http://www.peaceau.org/en/topic/the-african-peace-and-security-architecture-apsa
30 crisigroup.org.2018. China Expands Its Peace and Security Footprint in Africa.
31 Yun Sun. 2018. China's 2018 financial commitments to Africa: Adjustment and recalibration. 5 September. https://www.brookings.edu/blog/africa-in-focus/2018/09/05/chinas-2018-financial-commitments-to-africa-adjustment-and-recalibration/
32 amisom-au.org.2018. African Union Mission in Somalia. https://amisom-au.org/
33 un.org.2015. United Nations Peace and Development Trust Fund. https://www.un.org/en/unpdf/
34 Debelo, Asebe. R. 2017. The African Union's Peace and Security Partnership with China. 1 July. https://www.ssrc.org/publications/view/the-african-union-s-peace-and-security-partnership-with-china/
35 Fisher, Richard D. 2018. China Militarizes Its Influence in Africa.
36 Fredholm, M. 2012. The Shanghai Cooperation Organization and Eurasian Geopolitics: New Directions, Perspectives, and Challenges. Copenhagen: NIAS Press.
37 eng.mod.gov.cn.2019. Feature: Overview of 1st China-Africa Peace and Security Forum.17 July. http://eng.mod.gov.cn/news/2019-07/17/content_4846012.htm
38 Fisher, Richard D. 2018. China Militarizes Its Influence in Africa.
39 The head office of the Department of Defense and a synecdoche for the Department of Defense and its command center.
40 Seldin, J. 2021. China Eyes More Bases in Africa, US Military Official Says. 22 April. https://www.voanews.com/usa/china-eyes-more-bases-africa-us-military-official-says
41 Seldin, J. 2021. China Eyes More Bases in Africa, US Military Official Says.
42 uschina.org.2015. Unofficial Translation of the Counter-Terrorism Law of the PRC. December 27th. https://www.uschina.org/china-hub/unofficial-translation-counter-terrorism-law-peoples-republic-china
43 mg.co.za.2018. China's expanding military footprint in Africa. https://mg.co.za/article/2018-10-24-chinas-expanding-military-footprint-in-africa/
44 xinhuanet.com.2019. African military officer delegation starts weeklong visit to China. http://www.xinhuanet.com/english/2019-04/21/c_137996213.htm
45 Biryabarema, Elias. 2018. Ugandan soldiers to guard Chinese businesses after rash of robberies. 15 November.

https://www.reuters.com/article/us-uganda-crime/ugandan-soldiers-to-guard-chinese-businesses-after-rash-of-robberies-idUSKCN1NJ2JN

[46] chinaafricarealstory.com.2019. Chinese Lending to Africa for Military and Domestic Security purposes. 9 April. http://www.chinaafricarealstory.com/2019/04/chinese-lending-to-africa-for-military.html

Chapter 5 : United Nations Peacekeeping Missions in Africa

Background

On 25 October 1971, Albania's motion to recognize the PRC as the sole legal China was passed as General Assembly Resolution 2758 in the UN. It was supported by most of the communist states (including the Soviet Union) and non-aligned countries (such as India), but also by some NATO countries such as the United Kingdom and France. The Chinese leadership from the onset pursued a policy of non-participation in UN peacekeeping missions. The implementing of the policy was clear when China voted against a resolution to send troops to Guatemala and Macedonia in 1997 and 1999. In 1982 it was decided to make a financial contribution to the UN peacekeeping budget.

In 1988, China joined the UN Special Committee on Peace Missions and agreed to follow the traditional way of maintaining peace in post-conflict societies. The traditional way is based on three principles: impartiality, the non-use of force except for self-defense and the upholding of the mission's mandate. After the Tianmen

Square massacre in 1988 China endured a lot of criticism from the West, especially with respect to the principle of non-interference. The Chinese government viewed peacekeeping missions as interfering in the domestic affairs of other countries and this premise continued until Jiang Zemin became president in the 1990s. Jiang sought to restore China's international status through participation in UN peacekeeping missions.[1]

In 1991 and 1992, China sent observers to the UN missions in Cambodia and Haiti. These observers acted in an unofficial capacity and did not have a mandate to make active contributions. Nearly a decade passed before troops were deployed on active missions. The first one being the mission in East Timor in 2000.

China's diplomatic and economic relations with African countries rapidly increased in the 2000s. The establishment of more UN missions in Africa also meant that China could gain experience in peacekeeping missions and gain a favorable image among African countries. In 2003, China deployed troops to the UN Organization Stabilization Mission in the DRC (MONUSCO), and the following year to the UN Mission in Liberia (UNMIL).[2] In 2007, China deployed troops to the

UN African Union Hybrid Operation (UNAMID) in Darfur. It is argued that the protection of China's oil interests in Darfur was an incentive for participation in UNAMID.[3] In 2013, China for the first deployed combat troops to the United Nations Multidimensional Integrated Stabilization Mission in Mali (MINUSMA).[4]

Since 2014, China has been following the wider trend in peacekeeping missions, that is, to expand the UN's limited military capability to provide for drones, assault helicopters and armored vehicles equipped with cannons and machine guns. An example of this is the 1031 combat troops sent by China to the United Nations Mission in South Sudan (UNMISS) and a helicopter squadron to UNAMID.[5]

In 2015, China launched a UN peace and development trust and by the end of 2018, more than 11 million USD was allocated for use in security projects. Some of the funds will be used to train AU police and soldiers for peacekeeping, funding for specific missions, and supporting the AU's Silence the Guns initiative to stop violence and wars in Africa. To support these efforts 8000 Chinese soldiers are on standby and ready to be called up anytime. By the end of 2020, China was the second largest financial contributor to the UN peacekeeping budget and eleventh of all participating countries in terms of troop contributions (2,521 active troops by the end of 2020). Of the five permanent members of the Security Council, China's contribution is the largest. The contribution represents 25% of the total UN force. Chinese troops have also been deployed as police officers to maintain law and order and as security guards to guard facilities. Sharing knowledge with other contingents and learning new skills are some of the biggest benefits in peacekeeping participation.[6]

Motivations for China's Peacekeeping Missions

Peacekeeping gives China the opportunity to project an image as a responsible world player and a contributor to international stability. The opportunity to invest in the international system and reap economic and political rewards are also benefits. In the 1980s and 1990s, Chinese leaders moved away from Mao's revolutionary school of thought to one of development.

According to Wang Jingwu, dean of the Department of International Relations at China's National University of Defense in Beijing, participation in UN peacekeeping

---

missions is based on four principles. First, the Chinese concept of peace: China stands for an international political and economic order of peace and development. Peace is a prerequisite for development. The development of all countries in the world is included in the concept. Second, The Chinese point of departure. China emphasizes the fact that participation in UN peacekeeping missions is not a right to interfere in the domestic affairs of host countries. The rights and interests of host countries must be respected.

Third, Contributions. For the past decade, China has made the largest contribution to the UN budget for peacekeeping missions, and provided generous financial contributions to the China-UN peace and development fund, and deployed troops to the AU Standing Force. Fourth, Chinese power. Over the last few decades, China developed as one of the key players in UN peacekeeping missions and can rightly be regarded as the backbone of the UN Department of Peacekeeping.

Chinese political experts claim that China has developed its own set of characteristics for peacekeeping missions. In the media, it is known as peace missions with Chinese characteristics. One of the great features is Beijing's refusal to accept the responsibility to protect (R2P) principle. This principle means the host country must give permission before military intervention is undertaken and that military intervention should not threaten the sovereignty of the host country.[7]

There are further different categories of peace missions, namely traditional peace missions, monitoring mission areas, building peace in post-conflict societies, and restoring law and order. China initially only followed the traditional way of peacekeeping in accordance with mandates of the mission areas. As the challenges and needs of mission areas grew, it was decided to take an eclectic approach. Different ways of peacekeeping are now combined to maintain peace and security in a coordinated manner.

In the traditional way of peacekeeping missions, large contingent troops are deployed to mission areas in the aftermath of armed conflict. The troops are usually equipped with smaller weapons that are used as a deterrent to keep warring groups apart. In the traditional way of peacekeeping, all parties give permission for the deployment of troops, all parties are neutral in mediating disputes and outcomes, and all parties are committed to peace and the non-use of violence. Violence may only be used for self-defense and the protection of the mission's mandate. Peacebuilding involves restoring infrastructure destroyed in the conflict. It does not include major development projects, but involves the repair of bridges, power lines, water pipelines and the provision of medical assistance and equipment. In this regard, engineering and medical corps have already done great work to improve the infrastructure of the DRC, Liberia and the Sudanese.

Troops also reserve the right to enforce laws and ensure that citizens obey the laws. Since the late 2000s, members of China's peacekeeping police has been tasked with maintaining law and order in the streets of Monrovia and Bensonville in Liberia. A commitment to the economic and social development in post-conflict societies and the pursuit of permanent peace is part of the eclectic approach that China is pursuing.[8]

Consequences of China's Participation in African Peacekeeping Missions

According to Zhou Bo, a former director of the Department of Defense's Center for International Security,

China is a major player in UN peacekeeping missions in Africa. In an interview conducted in 2018, he claimed that peace missions help maintain good relations between China and Africa. China's peace missions bring direct benefit to African countries through the deployment of military and civilian personnel and indirect benefit through support and training to the AU 's Standing Force. China has previously provided military assistance to soldiers from Burundi and Uganda to facilitate their peacekeeping missions in Somalia.[9]

The lack of operational experience is a persistent problem for the Chinese military. However, participating in peacekeeping missions is an opportunity to cooperate with several other armies of the world in military operations other than direct warfare. In this way, knowledge is shared, new technology is exchanged and friendships are forged. From the government's point of view, peacekeeping missions are a means of gaining international status as a military power. Foreign Minister Wang Yi declared in 2020 that peacekeeping missions are a means to an end to China's foreign policy of peaceful coexistence and economic development.[10]

Notes

[1] Lanteigne, Marc and Miwa Hirono. 2012. *China's Evolving Approach to Peacekeeping* . London: Routledge.

[2] Miwa Hirono. 2018. *China and Peacekeeping* . London: Oxford Publishers.

[3] Contessi, Nicola P. 2010. Multilateralism, Intervention and Norm Contestation: China's Stance on Darfur in the UN Security Council. *Security Dialogue* , 41 (3): 323-44.

[4] peacekeeping.un.org.2021. MINUSMA Fact Sheet. https://peacekeeping.un.org/en/mission/minusma

[5] news.cgtn.com.2020. China and UN in graphics: A contributor to world peace. https://news.cgtn.com/news/2020-09-18/China-and-UN-in-graphics-A-contributor-to-world-peace-TPwjeqR1cs/index.html

[6] usip.org.2018. China's Evolving Role as a UN Peacekeeper in Mali. September. https://www.usip.org/sites/default/files/2018-09/sr432-chinas-evolving-role-as-a-un-peacekeeper-in-mali.pdf

[7] Borah, Jayshree. 2020. Peacekeeping With Chinese Characteristics. 25 September. https://thediplomat.com/2020/09/peacekeeping-with-chinese-characteristics/

[8] fmprc.gov.cn.2020. Position Paper of the PRC On the 75th Anniversary of the United Nations. https://www.fmprc.gov.cn/mfa_eng/wjdt_665385/2649_665393/t1813751.shtml

[9] Savkov, Nikita. 2020. China's Discourse and Interests Related to Its Role in UN Peacekeeping. *China Brief* , 20 (19): 25-30.

[10] Hey, Yin. 2019. China takes the lead in UN peacekeeping. 26 September. https://www.chinadaily.com.cn/a/201909/26/WS5d8bfa01a310cf3e3556d7f3.html

Chapter 6: Dimensions of China's Military Diplomacy in Africa

Arms Sales

Arms sales are currently an important element of China's military diplomacy in Africa. In the last number of years, the demand for Chinese weapons has increased due to low prices and the variety offered. The training that China provides in the use of weapons also makes it an attractive option. In another instance, weapons are sometimes exchanged for natural resources or offered as part of a deal to build infrastructure under the BRI.[1]

Several countries in Africa buy weapons from China, including the DRC, Gabon, Ghana, Namibia, Niger, Sierra Leone, Tanzania and Chad. Light weapons and ammunition have been provided on a large scale to liberation movements in the past, despite UN resolutions banning the sales of these weapons.[2] In recent decades, light weapons and ammunition have been sold to rebel groups and armies in war-torn and countries engaged in conflict. Countries that previously and currently purchase weapons and ammunition from China include, Côte d' Ivoire, the DRC, Libya, Somalia, Sudan and South Sudan.

There are also allegations that the Djibouti base is being used to distribute illegal weapons across Africa.[3]

In the period 2014-2018, America, Russia, France, Germany and China accounted for 75% of international arms sales. In terms of Chinese arms sales, Asia and Oceania were the largest buyers at 70% and Africa at 30%. Between 2009-2013 and 2014-2018, China's arms sales in Africa increased by 2.7%. Sub-Saharan African countries are the largest importers at 24%, while North Africa stands at 13%. In Africa, Russia's share is 49%, America 15%, France 7.8% and Germany 7.7%. From 2019 until today, China is the second largest arms supplier to Africa after Russia with a total sales of 19%. Russia is in first place with 36 percent and France in third place with 7.6 percent.

A feature for the period 2014-2018 was a growth in the demand for sophisticated weaponry such as unmanned attack vehicles and drones instead of conventional weaponry. China, for example, sold drones and satellite tracking devices to Nigeria in the country's fight against Boko Haram. America's strict control over sales of unmanned assault vehicles and drones offered China the opportunity to gain a stronger share in that market. In the period 2009-2013, China sold only 10 drones to overseas customers, but in the period 2014-2018, it increased to 153 in 13 countries. This includes several African countries.[4]

There are three periods that characterize the sale of Chinese weapons to Africa. The first coincides with China's economic reforms at home and the industrialization campaign of the late 1970s. The second coincides with the outward foreign policy of the 1990s and the third coincides with the introduction of the BRI in the mid-2010s. Arms sales are promoted through BRI-related projects. In North Africa, Algeria and Morocco bought Chinese weapons after China subsidized major infrastructure projects. Countries in Sub-Saharan Africa also buy weapons from China. Examples are Mali, Cameroon and Nigeria who buy light weapons and armored vehicles in the fight against terrorism.

In southern Africa, Tanzania is one of China's largest customers, mainly due to the two countries' strong bilateral relations and political solidarity. Before the start of the 21st century, none of these countries had purchased weapons from China. However, China is currently recruiting customers across Africa.[5]

Some of the low-cost weapons China sells to Africa include the Guizhou FTC-2000G supersonic fighter jet. The aircraft's engine is based on the Russian MIG-21 and has a modern radar system and glass cabin that can launch Chinese-made weapons. Sudan purchased 6 FTC-2000Gs in 2017. However, there is criticism of China's sales of low-cost weapons to Africa. An example is South Africa, which has been the largest arms manufacturer on the continent for decades and which views China's rising sales as a threat to the local arms-manufacturing industry. This is especially true in the manufacture of weapons developed specifically for the African terrain, for example armored and support vehicles.[6]

North Africa accounted for 74% of Africa's arms purchases for the period 2015-2019. Algeria has purchased 79% of all weapons making it the highest buyer in the region. An increase of 71% since 2010 and the 6th largest buyer of new weapons in the world for the period 2015-2019. The increase is viewed in the context of the Algeria's protracted conflict with Morocco, local political tensions and concerns over the conflict in neighboring Mali and Libya. For the period 2010-2014, Russia was the main supplier of arms to Algeria and maintained this position for the period 2015-2019. Algeria's arms purchases from Russia stood at 67%, followed by China at 13% and Germany at 11%.

Weapon imports for SSA stood at 26% for the period 2015-2019. In total, imports were 49% less than for the period 2010-2014 and the lowest since 1995-1999. The 5 largest arms importers in SSA were Angola, Nigeria , Sudan, Senekal and Zambia. The countries accounted for 63% of all arms imports in SSA. Angola at 27% was the largest arms importer and internationally in 42nd place. Although in a recession, Angola's arms imports were 20% higher in 2015-2019 than in 2010-2014.

China sells mostly small and light weapons to Sub-Saharan Africa countries. These include semi-automatic assault rifles, light machine guns, mortars and mortar launchers, hand grenades, landmines and handguns. In the last number of years, the demand for larger weapons has also started to increase, especially in areas where conflict and civil wars prevail. To meet the demand, the Chinese government began selling more advanced weapons to Africa. Nigeria, for example, has purchased the unmanned CH-3 drone and sophisticated VT-4 attack tank to assist the military in their fight against Boko Haram.

China's Party-Military Model in Africa

China's party-military model is one where the military is subordinate to the CCP. The model is in contrast to the multiparty democratic systems in Africa where the military is not an instrument in the hands of political parties to further their interests. Under African constitutions the military is only responsible to elected leaders. Mao Zedong stated that the party controls the military and the military must never be allowed to control the party. This rule defines the relationship between the CCP and the PLA. As China's relations with African armies grow, so does the party-military model. Two of the most important tools to promote the model are training and work-related programs.

The China-Africa Action Plan (2018-2021), for example, provides for the training of 60,000 African students in the foreseeable future. This is far more than the number of students applying for studies in the United States and the United Kingdom (UK). A further 50,000 professional training opportunities and government bursaries are made available to applicants from Africa. And lastly, there are about 5,000 openings for the training of professional military officials. That is 2000 more than the figures released in the 2015-2018 action plan.

The Chinese party-military model tends to improve networks and help create organizational structures. In this regard, interpersonal relationships between politicians, government officials, and military officers are key elements in building party structures. The Chinese party-military model is attractive to certain political parties in Africa, because the survival of the party depends on strong military presence, for example, Ethiopia, Libya and Sudan.

During the 18th Congress of the CCP in 2013, proposals were made on the restructuring of the military. The theme of the congress focused on absolute obedience of the military to the CCP. Three mechanisms were proposed for the restructuring of the military. First, the SMC exercises direct control over the military. This committee is responsible to the Politburo and has more executive power than the Department of Defense, which only acts in an advisory capacity.

Second, a network of political commissioners in the Political Department of the SMC is responsible for political and ideological training to the military. These commissioners carry the same rank and authority as the military commanders of each unit. The Political Department has the same authority as the chiefs of staff of military units and executes joint decisions on logistics, strategic planning and training.[7]

Third, the power is transferred to senior military leaders that sit on the CCP's highest decision-making bodies. This decision was taken to ensure the survival of the CCP. According to the party-military model, students and working officials can use China's professional military training programs to advance their careers on three levels. The first is the regional academies for cadets and junior officers, such as the Nanjing Military Academy, the Dalian Navy Academy and the Air Force's Aviation School in Jilin in northeastern China. Next are the control and staffing colleges in Nanjing and Shijiazhuang.

These colleges are responsible for the training of middle level officers. The majority of military students from Africa undergo training at the colleges. China's National University of Defense and National University of

Technology are the highest level and offer training for senior officers. More than 300 senior officers from countries around the world undergo training at these universities each year. Senior officers from Africa make up about 60% of the students.[8]

By the end of 2020, several African officials had attended China's institutions of political and military training. Angola, Algeria, Cabo Verde, Ethiopia, Eritrea, Guineau-Bissau, Mauritania, Mozambique, Rwanda, South Sudan and Tanzania all use various forms of Mao's model to connect the military with the ruling party. Furthermore, the Chinese military offers training for officers and senior civilian personnel, where they can experiment with the Chinese model to see if it is practically feasible in their own military environments.

Adjustments to the model can be made following practical applications. Some of the training centers include Kunming National Academy, Pudong College, and Nanjing Political College. Hundreds of militia and members of security companies have already received training in the colleges. Political parties in Africa, such as the Ruling Council for the Defense of Democracy and Forces in Burundi, have sent some of their members to colleges for training. These members currently perform civil protection services in Burundi.

Several versions of China's political-military schools exist in Africa. These schools reflect China and African countries' shared historical and ideological traditions. Schools include Uganda's Oliver Tambo Leadership Academy, a political-military school built on a former ANC military base, a political school in Tatek Ethiopia, the Southwest Africa's People's Organization (SWAPO) political school in Namibia and the ANC's political school in Venterskroon, South Africa.

In 2018, the CCP's internal liaison office made 45 million USD available for the construction of the Mwalimu Nyerere Leadership Academy in Tanzania. The academy's curriculum is based on the improvement of leadership skills, similar to those taught at Pudong College in Shanghai. Civilian and military cadres of former liberation movements in Africa, such as Angola, Botswana, Mozambique, Namibia, South Africa, Tanzania, Zambia and Zimbabwe, received training at the leadership academy for a period of three years. Most of the countries have entered into strategic partnerships with China. Training at the academy improves strategic decision-making, logistics management, and the development of leadership skills.[9]

The truth is that senior military leaders in Africa are not prepared to politicize their armies. Colonel Naison Ngoma of Zambia argues that the military and government should function separately and that politicization can easily take place if the two structures move too close to each other. Colonel Émile Ouédraogo of Burkina Faso claims that the military must be subordinate to civilian authority, obedient to the state and committed to political neutrality. Only if the three principles are followed can the military be truly professional.

The biggest factors hindering effective governance in the military include factions, political bias, and corruption. These factors are deeply rooted in the party structures of the CCP and have spilled over into the military due to the close connection between the party and military. Xi Jinping's call for the eradication of corruption in the military is a personal interference in military policy and causes the military to be politicized. Massive restructuring in the military has already resulted in the retrenching of more than 10,000 party members and 120 senior officers.

China's efforts to launch the party-military model in Africa are largely the result of strong ideological ties built during the freedom struggle. Some African leaders argue that Chinese models and doctrines were important in gaining independence and are still relevant in the current era for building relationships. On the other hand, there are military experts in Africa who argue that the main task of the military is the protection of the country's territorial sovereignty and should not serve as a means to achieve political goals. Despite this position, a basis is laid for the promotion of the party-military model in Africa.[10]

The Development Security Complex

Capacity building and human resource development represent a large part of China's overall Africa's security framework. The premise is that economic growth is a prerequisite for achieving peace and stability. One of the drivers of economic growth is the development of human resources. The assumption is that service delivery and a stable strategic and business landscape can be created, if capacity programs exist. The proposal on capacity generation is in fact one of the fundamental principles of a healthy market economy. China wants to ensure that workers in Africa build better capacity. This will help with the development of abilities, instincts, skills and resources, which are all usefull in a changing and competitive world. President Xi Jinping declared at the 2015 China-Africa Cooperation Forum in Johannesburg that China is ready to play an active role in Africa's development. According to Xi, capacity building is absolutely essential for promoting economic development, security and peace.

In China, development is considered a prerequisite for creating a secure political, economic and social environment. Development and security are interconnected and interdependent. Chinese leaders strongly believe that creating jobs for younger generations form the backbone of a healthy economy. Furthermore, it strengthens the security of the labor market and way of governing. Capacity building and vocational training have been an important part of China's security policy since the launch of the BRI. In some respects, it is more important than the sale of weapons, the deployment of peacekeeping troops, military training and other dimensions of military diplomacy.

The contributions that China makes to development

projects in Africa extend beyond programs to increase capacity in the security and military sectors. These include human resource programs for public officials, specialists in the agricultural sector, medical staff, journalists and other professions. Certain human resource programs have been developed specifically for the African market.[11]

Chinese leaders on many occasions expressed their views that security is needed for economic development. The Minister of Foreign Affairs, Yang Jiechi, stated in 2010 that development is the foundation for peace in Africa. Conflict and poverty go hand in hand and often form a vicious cycle. According to Chinese politicians the view security is based on two principles. The first principle is that an absence of conflict will lead to a safe environment. The second principle is more in line with reality and states that the origins of conflict in Africa can be traced to poor economic development.

Conflict can be prevented if jobs are created, poverty is alleviated and more development projects are launched. China is a major player in conflict resolution procedures, which contribute to economic and social development. In this regard, China supports the 2000 Brahimi report, which highlights the importance of economic and social development as key elements in building peace. The report abstains from focusing too much on peacekeeping, and rather highlights the importance of conflict resolution through mediation.[12]

The development security complex dates back to the industrialization campaign launched during the presidency of Deng Xiaoping. The plan was to accelerate economic growth, alleviate poverty and create jobs for the younger generation. The plan was successful in three ways; economic growth was raised to acceptable levels, new factories were built, which increased the process of industrialisation, and the population viewed the CCP as a legitimate party with strong leadership. The development of domestic security programs further increased the standing of the CCP among the population. Security also had an international dimension.

If China could develop joint security programs with neighbouring countries and international partners, it could lead to better cooperation and mutual security benefits. During the Cold War period, leaders in the CCP abstained from Western countries' focus on forming military alliances and engaging in an arms race. Security from the Chinese perspective focused on mutual trust and general interests. The perspective was strongly influenced by Jiang Zemin and Hu Jintao.[13]

Xi Jinping took the concept of security one step further by connecting security and development. Xi's synchronized and integrated connection between economic development and security is found not only in China's policies in the region, but also in Africa. Wang Jiechi, at the World Peace Forum in 2013, stated that successful diplomacy leads to successful economic development. He implied that Chinese diplomats have the right skills to promote peace and security in their dealings with foreign counterparts.

China's experience with domestic economic development and security lays the groundwork for promoting international peace and security.

The Integration of security and development is currently part and parcel of China's official African policy documents. China's African policy is an attempt to form a bloc of non-aligned African countries that support the establishment of a new international order. African countries view the prioritizing of economic development as important to obtain growth and building peace. That is why the Chinese

model of governance is preferred over Western countries'
focus on good government, democracy and human rights.
Angola, the DRC, both Sudans and Zimbabwe have
already applied some elements of the Chinese model in
their forms of governments.[14]

Wang Yizhou, a professor of International Relations at the
Beijing School of International Studies, argues that the
traditional way of peacekeeping has become obsolete.
Peace can only be achieved if the economies of countries
are developed in post-conflict situations. Since the mid-
2000s, China has been helping to restore basic
infrastructure and integrate communities in Angola, the
DRC, Liberia and Sierra Leone. Developing and building
peace are two concepts that are interlinked. In each of
the six meetings of FOCAC, development and stability is
prioritized over the Western concepts of democracy and
good governance.[15]

Chinese Security Contractors in Africa

Chinese security contractors have shifted their operations
increasingly to Africa in the last decade. In most cases,
the contractors work for Chinese state-owned companies
to secure oil and gas installations, rail networks, mines,

building sites and embassies. Since 2012, large numbers of Chinese workers have temporarily moved to Africa to work on development projects. By the end of 2018, almost one million Chinese workers moved to Africa to work on BRI projects. There are more than 10,000 Chinese companies in Africa, and about 2,000 state-owned companies. These companies generate almost 40 billion USD each year on construction projects.

The Chinese Academy of Social Sciences claims that 84% of BRI investments are made in medium- to high-risk countries. Between 2015 and 2017, there were 350 serious incidents that endangered the safety of Chinese companies and citizens. These include kidnappings, terrorist attacks, and xenophobia. Businesses are increasingly concerned about the safety of personnel and the safekeeping of facilities. Security contractors are requested to protect their property and show a greater presence around construction sites and industrial parks.

The Chinese military is not willing to get involved in the protection of facilities and the security of nationals abroad. This is largely due to the image they want to portray as professional soldiers and the failure to provide logistical support. On the other hand, Chinese leaders do not trust

African governments to protect their African interests which leads to a rise in the use of Chinese contractors. China has 5,000 registered security firms employing 4.3 million former military and police members. Of these firms, 20 are registered to work overseas, with an estimated 3,200 individual contractors. That is more than the 2,500 members of the Chinese military performing active overseas duties.[16]

The term private security contractor is misleading and inaccurate in the Chinese context. As a one-party state, the CCP requires all enterprises to be loyal to the party and party policy. A member of the CCP has to serve in the organizational structure of businesses with three to five employees. The directors of companies are not only valued party members but also the secretaries of their respective internal party structures. The state has the right to ownership of security firms or owns at least 51% of the capital investment.

The role of the CCP and the state bureaucracy in regulating the security sector is important, because the socialist market model is the indicator by which security objectives are formulated. For this reason, it is difficult to distinguish between private and public security. China passed a law in 1993 appointing only former members of the military as contractors in the public sector. In 2009, the law was amended so that contractors can also work in the private sector. The State Security Council is responsible for the administration of security services, which means that contractors are controlled by the state. [17] Research from the Overseas Security and Defense Research Center in Beijing states that contractors spend about 10 billion USD annually on securing businesses overseas.

Africa also offers golden opportunities for contractors. During the Chinese navy's anti-piracy operations in the Gulf of Aden and the Somali coast in 2008, Chinese contractors entered the African scene for the first time. Huaxin Zhong An and the Overseas Security Guardians have obtained government approval to place armed security guards on ships.

In order to gain greater international exposure, Chinese contractors modified their portfolios. Beijing DeWe Security Service, for example, signed a contract to secure Poly-GCL Petroleum Group Holdings gas plant in Ethiopia at a cost of 4 billion American dollars.

Shandong Haiwei Security Group protects state-owned mines in southern Africa. China's Overseas Security Group, a conglomerate of five firms, protects BRI projects in conflict areas, such as Somalia and Ethiopia. China Security and Technology Group protects land and sea transportation routes in the Gulf of Guinea, and the Lamu Port-South Sudan-Ethiopia Transport (LAPSSET) corridor. The local political climate and business landscape is first assessed before security services are offered. The friendlier and safer the environment, the greater the space in which contractors can move. In South Africa with its insecure and unstable political environment, contractors have very little room to maneuver.

They are often in partnerships with local contractors to demonstrate greater readiness and mobility. For example, Shandong Haiwei Security Group cooperates with Raid Private Securities of Durban to protect mines. In Kenya, contractors not only secure businesses but also help with training, providing technical skills and equipment. Chinese contractors are better trained than African security firms to perform work-related tasks.

In Sudan and South Sudan, the relationship with local security officials is very private. In 2012, members of the

VSS Security Group helped to rescue twenty nine Chinese oil workers from a plant in Sudan. In another incident in 2016, members of DeWe Security Service helped bring 300 oil workers to safety.[18]

Certain Chinese contractors recruit former members of Western militaries (veterans), who are then tasked to run the security company. For example, the London Overseas Security Services Group, registered in London, has a Western profile but caters to the needs of Chinese customers. These Western-based companies are however, criticized for their operations in conflict areas of the world. Frontier Services Group received a lot of criticism in the media for their operations in Somalia , South Sudan and the DRC.

Frontier Services Group was founded by Eric Prince, a former American navy marine and is owned by Citic, China's largest state-owned conglomerate. UN observers accused Prince in 2021 of supplying weapons to Khalifa Haftar, a military faction in Libya, to fight against government forces. This example shows that Citic used Frontier Services Group to make a financial profit.[19]

Chinese security contractors are also involved in suspicious operations that often have to do with the illegal use of weapons. In 2018, two Chinese citizens were arrested in Livingstone, Zambia for the illegal military training of a local security company. The training officers wore the same uniforms as those of Zambia's Department of Environmental Conservation. In neighboring Zimbabwe, two Chinese citizens were jailed for the shooting of a member of parliament's son. In Kenya and Uganda, contractors were arrested in 2019 and 2020 for the possession of illegal weapons and detection devices.[20]

In the last couple of years, African governments show a greater awareness to investigate suspected and irregular activities of Chinese contractors. Transparency and responsibility are two aspects that are scrutinized. Local communities also call for the investigation of security contractors around oil and gas plants. It is in these industries where large numbers of Chinese contractors are employed.

Strategic litigation is rapidly gaining ground in examining the transparency of security contracts. In 2020, the Kenya Law Society presented the legal basis of the contract between DeWe and the China Roads and Bridges Corporation (CRBC) before the court. This case refers to the security of the Standard Kenya Gauge Railway built by China. In June 2020, the Nairobi Court of Appeal ruled that the contract between CRBC and DeWe was illegal due to circumvention of rules for the purchase of materials and other goods. A Chinese CRBC manager was convicted of fraud and dismissed. The Zimbabwe Environmental Law Association (ZELA) obtained a court order in 2020, banning Chinese contractors from overseeing coal mining in Hwange National Park.

The court order also stated that all mining activities in the park should be stopped. Strategic litigation is now an effective tool to raise awareness of illegal Chinese activities. The Zimbabwean government is further obliged to release status reports from the Sengwa power station. The power station was built by China Gezhouba Group built for an astronomical amount of three billion American dollars. The security of the plant was entrusted to China Security Technology, which is involved in other contracts under suspicious circumstances. The litigants now understand that if the activities of security contractors are made public, it is easier for them to win cases in court.[21]

A look to the future

Demand for Chinese security contractors in Africa is expected to increase. One of the big reasons for this is that they are not seen as mercenaries, but offer work-related services. These include training, investments, risk management, and more effective customer service. A negative aspect is that Chinese contractors fail to provide accountability for their daily activities. China is Africa's largest trading partner and is sensitive to its image in Africa. Security contractors are now a means to improve the image and for this reason it is important that the Chinese government put measures in place to regulate the industry.

Some of the measures include, decoupling contractors from state-owned companies to reduce financial control over contractors. Contractors should be allowed to act as professional entities in their own right. It is further important that African governments and the AU evaluate the role and sustainability of contractors within the African security architecture. In view of the greater presence of contractors in Africa, African governments can play a supervisory, rather than a spectator role.

Furthermore, cooperation between local and Chinese contractors should be increased. After nearly three decades of renewed presence on the continent and long participation in peacekeeping, China has a good understanding of the security challenges facing African countries.

Notes

---

[1] Heath Timothy R. 2018. China's pursuit of overseas security. https://www.rand.org/content/dam/rand/pubs/research_repor ts/RR2200/RR2271/RAND_RR2271.pdf

[2] Andersson, Hilary. 2008. China is fueling war in Darfur:13 July. http://news.bbc.co.uk/2/hi/africa/7503428.stm

[3] Hendrix, Cullen S. 2020. Arms and Influence? Chinese arms transfers to Africa in context. 15 July. https://www.piie.com/blogs/realtime-economic-issues-watch/arms-and-influence-chinese-arms-transfers-africa-context

[4] sipri.org.2018. "Trends in International Arms Transfers, 2018", 31 March. https://www.sipri.org/sites/default/files/2019-03/fs_1903_at_2018_0.pdf

[5] Hendrix, 2020. Arms and Influence? Chinese arms transfers to Africa in context.

[6] Matthews, Ron and Colin Koh. 2021. The decline of South Africa's defense industry, Defense & Security Analysis, 37 (3): 251-273.

[7] idcpc.org.cn.2021. Secure a Decisive Victory in Building a Moderately Prosperous Society in All Respects and Strive for the Great Success of Socialism with Chinese Characteristics for a New Era. https://www.idcpc.org.cn/english/cpcbrief/19thParty/index.ht ml

[8] Bitzinger, Richard A. and James Char. 2020. Reshaping the Chinese Military: The PLA's Roles and Missions in the Xi Jinping Era. London: Routledge.

[9] sardc.net.2018. Mwalimu Nyerere Leadership School. 2 October. https://www.sardc.net/en/southern-african-news-features/mwalimu-nyerere-leadership-school/

[10] au.int.2015. 2nd FOCAC Summit: The 6th FOCAC Ministerial Conference Opens. December 3rd. https://au.int/en/pressreleases/20151203

[11] Song, Wei. 2019. Facilitating Industrialization in Africa: China's Aid and African Industrial Capacity Building. China Quarterly of International Strategic Studies, 5 (4): 577-599.

[12] Benabdallah, Lina. 2016. China's Peace and Security Strategies in Africa: Building Capacity is Building Peace? African Studies Quarterly, 16 (3-4): 17-34.

[13] Wu, Guogang. 2006. The Peaceful Emergence of a Great Power? Social Research, 73 (1): 317-344.

[14] Large, 2021. China and Africa: The New Era.

[15] Wang, Yizhou. 2018. Creative Involvement: The Transition of China's Diplomacy. London: Routledge.

[16] Arduino, A. 2020. The footprint of Chinese private security companies in Africa. March. https://static1.squarespace.com/static/5652847de4b033f56d2bdc29/t/5e7a733475a31172316a05d5/1585083189926/WP+35+-+Arduino+-+Chinese+Private+Security+Companies.pdf

[17] Nantulya, Paul. 2020. Chinese security contractors in Africa. 8 October. https://carnegietsinghua.org/2020/10/08/chinese-security-contractors-in-africa-pub-82916

Chapter 7: The Belt and Road Initiative (BRI)

The BRI is a development strategy proposed by the Chinese government and focuses on the connection of China by land and sea with the European mainland. The aim of the initiative is to build infrastructure, help economies to develop and provide investments to nearly seventy countries and international organizations in Asia, Europe and Africa. Xi Jinping proposed the BRI after official visits in 2013 to Indonesia and Kazakhstan.

The Chinese government is promoting the initiative to increase regional cooperation and to ensure a shared future for all the participating countries. Some observers view the BRI as an attempt by China to establish a China-centered trade network and then gain economic dominance on the routes. The target date for the completion of the project is 2049, which coincides with the 100th anniversary of the Republic of China.[1]

The original Silk Road dates back to the westward expansion of China's Han dynasty (206BC). The Han dynasty established trade networks with the Central Asian countries of Afghanistan, Kazakhstan, Kyrgyzstan, Tajikistan, Turkmenistan and Uzbekistan, as well as present-day India and Pakistan. The routes stretched over a distance of fourthousand kilometers to Europe. Central Asia was thus the center of one of the first waves of globalization that connected the East with the West. Valuable Chinese items, such as, silk, spices, and gems, moved westwards, while China received gold, minerals, ivory, and glassware. But the Christian Crusades, as well as the conquest of territories by the Mongols in Central Asia, were a setback for trade. In present day, Kazakhstan, Kyrgyzstan, Tajikistan, Turkmenistan and Uzbekistan are economically isolated from each other. Intra-regional trade represents only 6.2% of all cross-border economic traffic.[2]

Xi's dream with the BRI includes the establishment of a wide network of railways, energy pipelines, highways and border control posts, moving in a westerly direction through the former Soviet Republics and heading south to Pakistan, India and the rest of Southeast Asia. Such a network would increase the international use of the Chinese currency (Renminbi) and facilitate financial transactions between countries in Southeast Asia. The Asian Development Bank claims that there is an annual deficit of 800 million USD to finance projects in the region.

In addition to infrastructure projects, China plans to build fifty Special Economic Zones (SESs), modeled on the Shenzhen Special Economic Zone, which China completed in 1980. This economic zone was built to accelerate economic traffic in the area. In order to accelerate maritime trade, China further plans to build ports on the Indian Ocean part of the route.[3]

The BRI aims to give impetus to China's geopolitical and economic ambitions. An aggressive economic policy can help China create new markets to trade goods and deliver services. Observers view the BRI as one of China's main objectives to push the "Made in China 2025" strategy onto the world stage. At the same time, China aims to strengthen the economically, neglected western regions of the mainland. In broad terms, the leadership is determined to restructure the economy to improve the quality of life of middle-income groups. Such a move would contribute to a raise in salaries and greater emphasis on the manufacturing of higher quality goods and services.[4]

The BRI's Early Influence in Africa

The initiative has significant consequences for Africa. Hundreds of millions or perhaps even billions of dollars are made available for infrastructure and development in Africa. This is to connect Africa to the rest of the world. The agencies primarily responsible for financing, include the state-owned Silk Road Fund, the Chinese Development Bank and the Export-Import Bank of China (Exim). In addition, the Asian Infrastructure Investment Bank (AIIB) and the Shanghai New Development Bank provide financing to the BRI.[5]

At the China-Africa Cooperation Forum in 2018, President Xi Jinping emphasized the need for cooperation between the World Bank, the African Union (AU) Agenda 2063 and the UN's Sustainable Development Plan for Africa. The AU's Agenda 2063 is a strategic framework for the socio-economic transformation of Africa over the next 50 years. It builds and seeks to accelerate the implementation of previous and existing growth and development initiatives. African countries' desire to industrialize and connect their economies with the rest of the world is a major challenge. The BRI offers opportunities to overcome this challenge.

China has the knowledge and skills to help African countries achieve its economic goals.[6]

The President mentioned that trade between China and Africa is showing an annual growth and by the end of 2018 it was the highest in the world. China's total Africa imports and exports in 2018 stood at 204.19 billion American dollars. This is a year-on-year increase of 19.7% since 2011. China's exports to Africa increased to 104.91 billion American dollars. This is a year-on-year growth of 10.8% since 2018. China's imports from Africa stood at 99.28 billion USD in 2018, a year-on-year growth of 30.8%.[7]

The President remarked that a number of agreements were signed with leaders of Africa countries. The countries represent Africa in the west, east, south and the Indian Ocean. They are all important to expand China's geopolitical ambitions in Africa and the Indian Ocean. Xi signed an agreement with the leader of Senegal to extend the BRI to the westcoast of Africa. This cooperative agreement will serve as a motivation for other countries in the region to follow suit. In Rwanda, Xi signed a agreement with President Paul Kagame. The new railway line connecting Dar Es Salaam with Rwanda will facilitate trade and the flow of migrant workers between countries in the region.[8]

Agenda 2063 and the BRI

Africa's development priorities, such as, the AU's Agenda 2063, and local economic development programs are in harmony with the BRI's objectives. In fact, the BRI is an initiative aimed to mutually strengthen cooperation between China and Africa. During the China-Africa Cooperation Forum in 2018, the BRI was mentioned in the same breath as Agenda 2063 and individual projects. China's rhetoric of economic development resonates with African leaders and is important to promote regional development.[9]

Agenda 2063 is a set of initiatives proposed by the AU and currently in the implementation phase. The set of initiatives was adopted on 31 January 2015 at the 24th AU Heads of State Assembly in Addis Ababa. The call for such an agenda was made at the 21st General Meeting of the AU on 26 May 2013, 50 years after the establishment of the AU. The proposed objectives of the Agenda are economic development (including the eradication of poverty within one generation), political integration (specifically the establishment of a federal or Confederate United Africa), improvements in democracy and the rule of law, the pursuit of security and peace across the continent, the strengthening of cultural identity through "African Renaissance" - and pan-African ideals, gender equality and political independence from foreign powers.[10]

Agenda 2063 includes 15 flagship projects, which were identified as instrumental in achieving the following goals in all areas of development: A high-speed train network that can connect all capitals in Africa and commercial centers, the formulation of a strategy for transforming Africa's economy from a supplier of raw materials to one that can use its own resources, the establishment of Africa's own free trade area, the introduction of the AU passport and the removal of all visa requirements for its holders, the end of wars, civil conflicts, gender-based violence and violent conflict by 2025, the construction of new dams for water security, the establishment of a single African air transport market, the establishment of an annual African Economic Forum, the establishment of a set of financial institutions, namely an African Investment Bank, a Pan-African Stock Exchange, an

African Monetary Fund and an African Central Reserve Bank, the creation of an African digital data network, the development of a comprehensive African space research strategy, the establishment of a digital University for distance-based teaching, cooperation on cyber security, the building of a museum that can preserve Africa's cultural heritage and promote pan-Africanism and the compilation of Encyclopedia Afrikana as an authoritative resource for the authentic history of Africa and its people.[11]

The first ten-year implementation plan of Agenda 2063 (2014-2023), in conjunction with the AU's Infrastructure Development Program and Africa's Integrated Maritime Strategy 2050, forms the basis for the realization of the BRI on the African continent.[12]

The AU is working closely with China to promote Africa's development. In 2015, Li Keqiang delivered a speech on collaboration with African partners at the AU's headquarters.

Various projects on cooperation were identified, some of them extensions from previous cooperation projects proposed at FOCAC. The projects are infrastructure development, industrialization, financial integration and economic development.[13] At the end of 2020, 43 African countries registered for the BRI, including the AU.[14]

The establishment of infrastructure and trading networks are essential elements of the BRI. The Suez Canal and Mediterranean sea provide direct access to countries in North Africa, thereby increasing the strategic importance of the region. North Africa is also in close proximity to Europe, which facilitates the flow of Chinese goods and services to European markets.

With the exception of Mauritania, all North African countries signed BRI cooperation agreements with China.[15] The BRI integrates well with the goals of North African countries and that is to improve economic ties with Europe and Sub-Saharan Africa. North African economic development is limited by a lack of interregional trade. Trade between countries in the region stands only at 16%, in comparison to 19% in South America and 51% in Asia. For example, trade between Algeria and Morocco stands at 4.8% and this is due to ineffective lines of communication and poor trade facilitating mechanisms.

The African Free Trade Area (AfCFTA) and infrastructure such as the Trans-African Highway can speed up interregional trade and alleviate other problems that may arise as a result of poor trade policies.

Morocco is seeking closer ties with Sub-Saharan African countries and signed trade deals with Nigeria, Benin, Liberia and Niger. In another positive step, Morocco successfully joined the Economic Community of West African States (ECOWAS) in 2017. Tunisia joined the Common Market for Eastern and Southern Africa (COMESA) in 2018.

China sees the establishment of a trans-Saharan trade network as a key objective to promote trade in the Sahara. Egypt has always been important to China because of the Suez Canal, Egypt's influence in the Arab world, (100 million people) and strong trade policies.[16]

Nigeria joined the BRI in 2018 after a very succesful infrastructure and industrial projects exhibition was held in Abuja. Some of the projects include the Abuja-Kaduna Railway, the Abuja Mass Rail Transit (MRT), the new terminal at the Nnamdi Azikiwe International Airport, Port Harcourt International Airport, Lekki deep sea port, and the Lagos-Ibadan railway. BRI infrastructure development projects have already changed the lives of thousands of Nigerians. For example, the Kaduna-Abuja railway line is now a major mode of transport for businessmen that commute from Abuja to Kaduna, the industrial heartland of Nigeria. Hundreds of Chinese companies that manufacture different products and deliver a wide array of services, are currently changing the Nigerian economic landscape.[17]

The countries in East Africa (Djibouti, Ethiopia, Kenya, Rwanda, Uganda and Tanzania), are strategically important on the maritime route. These countries have ports and are viewed as gateways to East Africa and down the coast. Large-scale BRI infrastructure projects, for example, railways, highways, airports, power stations and telecommunications networks are completed, while others are still under construction. The BRI presents these countries with the opportunity to become part of the global economic trade system. The BRI already has a domino effect on countries in the region, because of economic benefits and closer trading ties with China.

At FOCAC 2015 delegates agreed that the building of infrastructure could speed up Africa's industrialization process. This point was further China emphasized by China in G20 meetings. A study by the UN Economic Commission found that East Africa's annual exports could increase by as much as 192 million USD with the succesful launching of BRI projects.

The railway line connecting Mombassa with Nairobi, the largest investment in Kenya since independence, is a flagship BRI project in East Africa. The electric railway from Addis Ababa to Djibouti, is another example. The port of Djibouti is a strategically important trade hub for Ethiopia. Seventy percent of the country's total imports and exports are handled at the port.[18] The port handles about one million cargo containers and seven million metric tons of cargo each year.

By the end of 2020 revenue earned from trading at the port contributed almost four billion USD to Ethiopa's GDP. The Ethiopia-Djibouti railway is another BRI project completed. This line facilitates the transportation of goods and services from industrial areas to Djibouti. There are currently 14 industrial projects being developed in the region.

In Sudan there is the Khartoum oil refinery and in Eritrea the Hirgigo power plant, which are significant economic boosters for their countries. Further south is the Mombassa-Nairobi railway, which is currently extended to Uganda, South Sudan, Burundi and the DRC. This railway line will help to promote economic integration and development in the region. The maritime route will finally connect Djibouti, Sudan, Mauritania, Senegal, Ghana, Nigeria, Gambia, Guinea, Sao Tome and Principe, Cameroon, Angola and Namibia. These ports are spread out all across Africa. The final ark of the route will connect Walvis Bay in Namibia with Chinese-controlled port enclaves in Mozambique, Tanzania and Kenya, before moving on to Gwadar in Pakistan.[19] The Southern African Development Community (SADC) has partnered with the BRI to implement its industrialization strategy. Infrastructure development is important for both groups to speed up development in Africa.

During the fourth SADC Industrialization week held in August 2019 in Dar Es Salaam, senior officials stated that the BRI could connect the SADC with other development projects in the region.[20] The SADC's industrialization strategy focuses on the development of agro-processing, the refining of minerals and medical preparation. The BRI can help build infrastructure in Tanzania, the DRC, Mozambique and South Africa. These countries were identified for their strategic location and the leading role they play in promoting trade in the regions.[21]

South Africa has traditionally been in a strong position to serve as a gateway to Africa's business and financial markets. Policy documents were drawn up by the Department of International Relations and Cooperation to market South Africa's business potential. The BRI, however, dealt a serious blow to South Africa's ambition to serve as the leading economy on the continent. The argument is that the BRI is damaging South Africa's reputation and foreign policy identity on the continent.

At the heart of South Africa's foreign policy is a deep recognition of its interconnectedness with Africa's dreams and visions.

The country's admission to BRICS in 2010 meant, among other things, that South Africa, due to its strong leadership on the continent, could represent Africa in this important global economic grouping. South Africa's foreign policy players have indeed marketed the country as the gateway to Africa. With the arrival of the BRI however, cracks began to show in the montage of BRICS, to such an extent that the country could not overlook its partnership with China. It is important to note that South Africa's support for the BRI depends on the availability of networks and alternative options for economic growth. On a positive note, analysts are of the opinion that the BRI will also be favorable for South Africa in the long run. The country supports Agenda 2063 and the general objectives of the BRI. All countries in Africa can ultimately benefit from the BRI.

Summary of the BRI in Africa

China has embarked on large-scale infrastructure building projects in the world over the last two decades and Africa is no exception. Eversince the going out policy was announced in the mid 1990s, the Chinese government has used all possible means to influence the political and economic will of African leaders. In 2000, FOCAC was established and more issues of economic importance were put on agendas. The African leg of the BRI was announced during FOCAC 2015, only two years after the formal launch of the BRI. The initiative focuses not only on building infrastructure, but also on improving interpersonal relationships, exchanging knowledge, solidarity with the Chinese way of governance, value systems, ideology and creating a new set of international norms and standards. The ideal of building a common future with identical values and interests is a key feature of the BRI's international marketing campaign.

Notes

[1] Jones, L. and J. Zeng. 2019. Understanding China's 'Belt and Road Initiative': beyond 'grand strategy' to a state transformation analysis. *Third World Quarterly*, 40 (8): 1415-1439.

[2] Chatzky, A. and J. McBride. 2020. China's Massive Belt and Road Initiative. https://www.cfr.org/backgrounder/chinas-massive-belt-and-road-initiative

[3] Jones, L. and J. Zeng. 2019. Understanding China's 'Belt and Road Initiative': beyond 'grand strategy' to a state transformation analysis.

[4] Chatzky, A. and J. McBride. 2020. China's Massive Belt and Road Initiative.

[5] Risberg, P. 2019. The give-and-take of BRI in Africa. 8 April. https://www.csis.org/give-and-take-GPI -africa

[6] Belt and road forum.org. 2019. Xi Jinping Chairs and Addresses the Leaders Roundtable of the Second Belt and Road Forum for International Cooperation. 28 April. http://www.beltandroadforum.org/english/

[7] english.mofcom.gov.cn. 2019. Statistics on China-Africa trade in 2018. 26 January. http://english.mofcom.gov.cn/article/statistic/lanmubb/AsiaAfrica/201901/20190102831255.shtml

[8] Tiezzi, S. 2018. China's Belt and Road makes inroads in Africa. 31 July. https://thediplomat.com/2018/07/chinas-belt-and-road-makes-inroads-in-africa/

[9] Alden, C., E. Sidiropoulos and YS Wu. 2017. China's Belt and Road Initiative: Where does Africa fit? https://saiia.org.za/research/china-s-belt-and-road-initiative-where-does-africa-fit/

[10] Bialostocka, O. and T. Simelane. 2016. *New African thinkers: Agenda 2063. Drivers of change* . Pretoria: HSRC Press.

[11] Adejumobi, S. and A. Olukoshi. 2019. *The African Union and new strategies for development in Africa* . Illinois: Cambria Press.

[12] Demissie, AM Wiegelen X. Tang. 2016. *China's Belt and Road Initiative and its implications for Africa* . Nairobi: WWF Publishers.

[13] Ndzendze, B. and D. Monyae. 2019. China's Belt and Road Initiative: Linkages with the African Union's Agenda 2063 in historical perspective. *Transnational Corporations Review,* 11 (1): 38-49.

[14] Hakeenah, N. 2020. China's Belt and Road Initiative, AfCTFA to anchor Africa's economy. 11 April. https://theexchange.africa/countries/china-belt-road-initiative-afcfta-africa-economy/

[15] White and Case.com. 2018. Belt and Road in Africa. 7 February.
https://www.whitecase.com/publications/insight/belt-and-road-africa

[16] Kfir, I. 2019. Understanding the BRI in Africa and the Middle East. 13 February.
https://www.aspistrategist.org.au/understanding-GPI -africa-middle-east /

[17] Vanguard.com. 2020. How China's Belt and Road Initiative affects Nigeria, Africa. January 28th.
https://www.vanguardngr.com/2020/01/how-chinas-belt-and-road-initiative-affects-nigeria-africa/

[18] Belt and roadnews.com. 2019. Role of GPI on the Economic integration in Eastern Africa. 15 May.
https://www.beltandroad.news/2019/05/15/the-role-of-GPI -on-the-economic-integration-in-eastern-africa /

[19] White and Case.com. 2018. Belt and Road in Africa. 7 February.

[20] Xinhuanet.com.2019.Southern Africa bloc links with China's GPI over industrialization strategy. 5 August.
http://www.xinhuanet.com/english/africa/2019-08/05/c_138283451.htm

[21] Nyongesa, G. 2019. Region in Africa sees BRI as a way to prosper. 23 August.
http://www.chinadaily.com.cn/a/201908/23/WS5d5f3ad2a310cf3e35567720.html

Chapter 8: Case Studies of Military Diplomacy in Africa

Angola

China's ties with Angola dates back to the support of the National Front for the Liberation of Angola (FNLA), the National Union for the Total Independence of Angola (UNITA), and the People's Movement for the Liberation of Angola (MPLA).[1] These three freedom movements all waged a revolutionary war for independence from Portugal. The freedom movements viewed the Cultural Revolution in China as a struggle for freedom and accepted China's military aid. The fight for freedom was also influenced by Cold War Politics.

The MPLA received aid from China in the early 1960s, but the situation changed when the OAU decided to recognize the FNLA and UNITA as legitimate liberation movements. China stopped supporting the MPLA and started to deliver military aid to the FNLA and UNITA. The FNLA leader, Holden Roberto, met with Chinese Foreign Minister, Chen Yi, in 1963 in Nairobi, Kenya and agreed to supply most of the FNLA's weapons. In 1964, Jonas Savimbi, the chairman of the CCP, met Mao Zedong and Prime Minister

Zhou Enlai in Beijing. Savimbi in subsequent visits to Beijing received training in guerrilla warfare and the ideology of Maoism. With the end of the Cultural Revolution in the early 1970s, Chinese military advisers started to provide training to the MPLA. The military assistance was however short-lived, because of the MPLA's decision to align with the Soviet Union as political partner. China stopped providing assistance to the MPLA and decided to support the FNLA and UNITA. In 1974, the FNLA received 450 tons of weapons from China and instructors stationed in Zambia assisted in training FNLA rebels.[2]

The MPLA came to power in 1975. China initially refused to recognize Angola's independence, and formal diplomatic relations between Beijing and Luanda were not established until 1983. In the early 1990s, Chinese weapons and ammunition were transported from Zaire to UNITA-controlled areas in Angola. Angolan government forces launched an attack on UNITA in April 1993 and seized a big consignment of Chinese-made weapons. A 1993 US intelligence report showed that Type 72 anti-personnel mines in the consignment was manufactured in

China. The Chinese embassy in Luanda denied that any weapons were sold to UNITA.[3]

Since the start of the 21st century, there are regular contacts between officers of the Chinese and Angolan militaries. In 2004, China signed a 6 million USD agreement to build a training facility for the Angolan military. A separate agreement to upgrade Angola's military communications system followed in 2005. The installation of the system cost 100 million USD.

China's military aid to Angola aims to gain more legitimacy in the eyes of the Angolan government. China was accused in the 1990s of selling arms to UNITA and not loyal to the MPLA. The older guards in the Angolan government still accuse China of disloyalty to the MPLA, because all three liberation groups were supported in the freedom struggle.

In 2004, a strategic partnership with the government of President Jose Eduardo dos Santos was signed. The partnership was upgraded in 2015 to a comprehensive strategic partnership that provides for stronger military relations. In 2010, China offered to provide training to military personnel and incorporate elements of the PLA's organizational structure into the Angolan military.

In 2019, Angola started negotiations with China to build military infrastructure in the country and create logistical channels for the ordering and delivery of arms and ammunition. The sharing of technical knowledge and training of officers were also prioritized. The Angolan government believes that increased military cooperation can further strengthen the two countries' relationship. Understanding China's military structure will help the Angolan military to develop and increase its professionality.[4]

With respect to military hardware, Angola ordered 6 Hongdu JL-8 (Nanchang JL-8) planes in 2020. The approximate delivery date is before the end of 2022. The Hongdu JL-8 is a two-seater training aircraft and light attack aircraft that is manufactured by Nanchang Aircraft Manufacturing Corporation.[5]

The MPLA uses the party-military model of Mao Zedong to consolidate relations between the government and the military. The main reason for this ideological indoctrination is to ensure loyalty to the party. Angola's president João Lourenço is a former political commissioner who received his military training in the Soviet Union.[6]

The DRC

China's relations with the DRC dates back to 1960, the year when the DRC (Léopoldtville) gained independence from Belgium. From 1971 to 1997, the DRC was known as Zaire.[7] After the end of the first civil war in 1997, the name was changed back to the DRC. The Prime Minister of China, Zhou Enlai, during his visit to the DRC conveyed his personal congratulations to the newly elected government and Prime Minister Patrice Lumumba. From 1972 until Mobutu's government was overthrown by Laurent-Désiré Kabila in 1997, there were 16 reciprocal visits by Chinese and DRC officials. During the 1960s, the government of Mao Ze Dong provided limited military support to rebel forces to overthrow the government of Mobutu.[8]

China has been an active participant in the UN's Stabilization Mission in the DRC (MONUSCO) since the 2000s and has already sent several contingents to assist with conflict management and peacebuilding. Peacekeeping troops work with engineers to build roads and are also assisting with other construction projects. In recent years, China has also been training DRC military officers, sharing knowledge and technology, and arranging mutual visits by high-ranking military officers. Military relations were further strengthened with the construction of the Colonel Tshatshi military base in Kinshasa. The base is currently the headquarters of the DRC's military (FARDC). [9] The base was erected in memory of Joseph-Damien Tshatshi, a military commander loyal to the regime of Joseph-Désiré Mobutu. Tshatshi was killed by rebel forces in 1966 during the Kisangani uprising. [10]

In 2018, the Chinese military helped build a naval base in the coastal town of Banana. [11] The town is the location of the DRC navy's first regional base. Projects are also underway to expand the fleet's operational capabilities and visibility in specific areas. Kalemie is a town located on the western shore of Lake Tanganyika. The navy's second regional base is located in the town. The task of the navy is to stop rebel forces infiltrating the DRC from Uganda across Lake Tanganyika.

The navy's third regional base is located in Goma. The town is on the northern shore of the Kivu lake. The area around Goma and the eastern parts of the DRC is home to rebel groups, such as the Lord's Resistance Military

(LRA), the Democratic Forces for the Liberation of Rwanda (FDLR) and the M23 group.[12] North Kivu is considered a focal point of the conflict in the DRC. China has been sending peacekeepers to North Kivu since the mid-2000s to bring stability and peace. The Chinese base is in Goma. The navy's fourth regional base is in Mbandaka in the northwestern part of the country.[13] The fleet of the DRC is a brown water or river fleet. This means that patrols and military operations are carried out in littoral zones. China has sold eight Shanghai Type 062 gunboats to the Mobutu government.[14]

The Type 062 gunboat was developed and built in the 1950s. This unsophisticated boat was mounted with a 66-57mm rifle. A total of 30 of these boats served until the late 1990s. Apart from the DRC, the type 062 gunboat was also sold to Albania, Bangladesh, Egypt, North Korea, Pakistan, Sierra Leone, Sri Lanka, Tunisia and East Timor.[15] By the end of 2018, only 2 of the boats were operational due to poor maintenance.

A Chinese military base was established at Kamina in 2008. The base is in the southern part of the country. By the end of 2017, the first group of the Congolese army's counter-reaction unit had been trained.[16]

Mozambique

Mao Ze Dong established diplomatic and military relations with FRELIMO of Mozambique in the 1960s. During that time, Mozambique was engaged in a struggle for independence from Portugal. Chinese soldiers trained FRELIMO fighters, in the tactics of guerrilla warfare. The first president of Mozambique, Samora Machel, was a proponent of guerrilla warfare and praised the Chinese government for training FRELIMO fighters.

However, on the political front, Mozambique moved closer to the Soviet Union and in 1977 Marxism-Leninism was adopted as political ideology. Despite solidarity with the Soviet communist ideology, China maintained stable and friendly relations with Mozambique. With the Great Famine in 1983, China provided financial and material aid. [17] During the civil war from 1975 to 1992 between FRELIMO and RENAMO, China's military assistance to the government of President Joaquim Chissano was limited. FRELIMO received most of their weapons from Russia and other communist countries. In diplomatic terms , it was a period of détente. After the end of the civil war, the political climate in Mozambique was still unstable for many years and violence flared up sporadically in areas controlled by RENAMO . China was unwilling to engage economically in Mozambique and was waiting for some stability. Mozambique's relationship with the Russian government of Boris Yeltsin was also strong in the 1990s. Russia has supplied military hardware such as tanks and fighter jets to Mozambique. Although both China and Russia followed Marxist-Leninist ideology and had communist governments, Mozambique's solidarity with Russia was stronger.

The friendship between Chissano and Yeltsin was a telling example of the strong bond between communist leaders. Jiang Zemin's foreign policy has focused on improving relations with Western powers and little attention has been paid to developing countries. Veterans and FRELIMO party members are struggling to define relations with China in new terms. The Chinese government also has a problem understanding the political will and goals of Mozambican leaders.

Many of the senior members in the current Mozambican government received their training in Russia and were trained in that country's ethics, norms and values. For these members, it is a challenge to identify with the CCP's policy. However, the terms of China's cooperation with Mozambique are still being negotiated, also in the area of security and military aid.[18]

In 2007, a military aid protocol was concluded between China and Mozambique. The protocol highlighted the importance of military cooperation between the two countries. Mechanisms have been put in place that can promote military cooperation. The main objective was to find solutions to Mozambique's future security and defense challenges. As part of the effort, the Chinese government offered $ 1.5 million to upgrade the Mozambican army. Most of the money was used for the renovation of military departments and facilities.[19]

Since the end of 2017, Mozambique's northern Cabo Delgado province is under constant attack by Islamic extremists. Although China's local economic and trade projects are not affected by the attacks, Chinese leaders are deeply concerned that the conflict may threaten China's interests. The Chinese government is willing to provide military assistance if requested.[20] Mao's party military model is also applicable in Mozambique. Senior leaders of the military hold positions in the Central Committee of FRELIMO and the Political Commission. The latter is an inner circle of FRELIMO's Central Committee. FRELIMO uses hundreds of experienced party and military veterans to educate the community in the principles of socialism. Just like in Angola, this is done to ensure loyalty to the party.[21]

Sudan

Sudan was one of the first African countries to recognize the PRC in the late 1950s. It was also the beginning of the two countries' official relations.[22] Sudan began buying weapons from China during the reign of Jaafar Nimeiry (1969-1985). This included anti-personnel and landmines.[23] Following the civil war in Mozambique and the border war in Angola-Namibia, the UN adopted a resolution in 1993, which made the sale of landmines to African countries illegal. For many years after the end of conflicts in Africa, landmines were still deactivated, but not before hundreds of lives were claimed.

During the reign of Omar al-Bashir (1993-2019), formal contracts for the sale of arms were signed. As relations between China and Sudan strengthened, large oil concessions were awarded to Chinese companies. The American oil company Chevron discovered oil in the Upper

Nile area in 1977 and the first well was sunk in 1978. Sudan's largest oil reserves are located in the Muglad and Melut Rift Valleys in the south of the country. The Chinese government had to respect the principles of non-interference, territorial integrity, and non-aggression, before oil concessions were granted.[24]

Sudan purchased mostly older weapons from Russia, Hungary and the Czech Republic. In the first major arms deal, SCUD missiles were sold to the al-Bashir government worth 200 million USD. The Sudanese Foreign Minister, Dr. Mustafa Osman Ismai, arranged for the missiles to enter Sudan from Iraq.[25] The SCUD missiles are very inaccurate and have been used in Middle Eastern wars since 1970. Saddam Hussein used the missiles against the Kurds in the north of the country in an attempt to purge Iraq of this ethnic group. During the Iran-Iraq war of 1980-1988, hundreds of missiles were fired by both countries at each other.

It was not until the 1991 Gulf War that the international community took notice of the missiles . The George W. Bush administration classified the missiles as weapons of mass destruction and UN inspectors visited depots and showed the missiles to the world.[26]

Several African countries experienced political instability and civil wars during the period, for example Angola and Mozambique. Large quantities of weapons and ammunition were purchased from foreign suppliers to continue the military struggle. During the communist revolution, Mao Zedong declared that political power is obtained from the barrel of a gun. This slogan was used by freedom movements to take up arms and fight for independence.

Freedom fighters such as Robert Mugabe of Zimbabwe, Samora Machel of Mozambique, Holden Roberto of the FNLA and Joseph-Désiré Mobutu of the DRC used the slogan to inspire soldiers to keep on fighting.

With the takeover of Omar al-Bashir in 1989, there was a new interest in the purchase of Chinese weapons. al-Bashir had a personal relationship with Chinese leader Jiang Zemin and negotiated arms purchases for Sudan.[27] Former Sudanese Prime Minister and religious leader Sadiq al-Mahdi (1966-67; 1986-89) opposed the purchase of Chinese weapons.

Mahdi was still actively involved in politics at the time, arguing that Chinese weapons would contribute to divisions among members of the ruling National Islamic

Front (NIF).[28] Progressive party members in the NIF argued that arms purchases would strengthen the country's military position in the region. The decision was made to buy Chinese weapons due to low prices and China's development of the oil industry in Sudan.[29]

Arms purchases in the 90s included ammunition, tanks, helicopters, and fighter jets. China has supplied Sudan with 50 Harbin Z-5 helicopters, hundreds of 82mm Type 53 mortars and 120mm Type 55 mortars.[30] The Harbin Z-5 is a Chinese variant of the Russian Mil Mi-4 piston valve propelled helicopter. The first flight was in 1958 and mass production began in the 1960s. Apart from the shipment to Sudan, the helicopter was also sold to countries in the Middle East, Pakistan and Iran. A total of 558 Z-5s were built. Production of the Z-5s stopped in the early 90s. By the end of 2019, the inventory of the Sudanese air force showed that no new Chinese helicopters had been purchased. Sudan had 43 Mil Mi-24 Russian combat helicopters at the end of 2020.[31]

The 82mm type 53 mortar was originally manufactured in Russia as the M-37 or 82-BM-37. The mortar was used in various wars and conflicts in Central Asia, the Middle East and Russia. It was also exported to Africa where it was used in civil wars and freedom struggles. NORINCO redesigned the M-37 with a lighter base plate and a device that prevents misfires.[32] The 120mm Type 55 is a highly explosive mortar that shoots deadly fragments when it explodes. The tail is also stable when launched. The Chinese version is an redesign of the Russian 120mm OF-843B mortar. This mortar was an improvement of the type 53 M1943 mortar.

By the end of 1997, China supplied Sudan with the following weapons: First, 105mm recoilless guns, type 75, developed for the Chinese military in the mid-1970s. It is mounted on a 4x4 light four-wheel drive vehicle and is designed to engage light self-propelled, direct or indirect fire at enemy positions.[33]

Second, 122mm M-30 type 54-1 howitzers developed by NORINCO and based on the Russian 122mm howitzer M1938 (M-30). It is almost completely identical to the Russian model, except for smaller mechanical parts. The howitzer was the first large caliber artillery weapon manufactured by China and production began as early as 1953. It is not known how many of the weapons were delivered to Sudan.[34]

Third, T-59 combat tanks which is a modified version of the Russian T-55A model. The first tanks were manufactured in 1963. More than 10,000 of the tanks were manufactured until production stopped in 1985. About 5,500 of the tanks were used for exercises and wars in Afghanistan and the border conflict between China and India. The chassis and turret formed the basis for the development of the types 69 and 79 tanks. Production of the tanks stopped in 2000 with an estimated 3,000 of the types 59- I and 59- II still listed in inventories of armies around the world. During the Second Sudanese Civil War from 1983 to 2005, the government used the T-59 to attack the strongholds of rebel groups.

From 2010 to 2016, Khartoum also received several Type 85- II M (designated as Al-Bashier in the Sudanese Military-TASS) and Type 59D from China. The Type 85- II tank is mobile, adapted to desert conditions, has a top speed of 57km/h and an operational range of 480km. The tank is equipped with a smooth-bore 125mm 2A46M rifle, a 7.62mm type 59T coaxial machine gun and a type 12.7mm type 54 heavy machine gun. According to the military balance sheet of the Institute for Strategic Studies (IISS), Sudan had 465 operational tanks in 2016.

These include, 20 American M60A3, 60 Chinese type 59/59D, 305 Russian T-54/55, 70 Russian T-72M1 and 10 Chinese type 85- II m tanks.[35]

In 1997, Sudan bought 6 Chengdu F-7s, which are similar to the Russian MiG-21. The licensed version of the aircraft is the Chengdu J-7 and the export product is the F-7. The aircraft is equipped with infrared launcher air-to-air missiles and designed for short-range air strikes. Production of the J-7 discontinued in 2013. The newer model is the JF-17 purchased by armies in Asia. Large quantities of J-7s are still used by the Chinese Air Force. By the end of 2020, Sudan had 20 F-7s and 6 F6s. China also sold the Nanchang Q-5 to Sudan.

Fourth, the Type 69 85mm rocket-powered projectile launcher (RPG) manufactured by NORINCO. This model is the Chinese version of the Russian RPG -7, first used in 1972. The type 69 RPG series has been replaced by modern anti-tank weapon systems such as Type 89 and 08.

An inspection by Human Rights Watch into the state of Sudan's weapons in 1997 revealed large quantities of type 69 85mm in storage sites across the country.[36]

In 2004, the UN imposed a ceasefire against Sudan to stop ethnic violence in Darfur. China, however, continued to supply weapons to Janjaweed civilian forces. Human Rights Watch singled out China as the biggest violator of the arms embargo for the period 2004-2006.[37] The war in Darfur was a violent conflict between the Sudan Liberation Movement, (SLM) and Justice and Equality Movement (JEM) on the one hand and government forces and the militant Janjaweed on the other.[38]

The conflict began in 2003 when JEM rebel groups accused the government of violence against the non-Arab section of the population. Rebel groups attacked oil installations and government facilities, after which a campaign of ethnic cleansing was launched. This led to the deaths of hundreds of thousands of civilians. Charges of genocide, war crimes, and crimes against humanity have been filed against Sudanese President Omar al-Bashir at the International Criminal Court in The Hague. Chinese aid was not limited to the supply of weapons and ammunition. According to a report by Amnesty International, Chinese trucks were used to pick up civilians during the 2004 Darfur massacre. It happened in the town of Wadi Saleh.[39]

South Sudan

The South Sudan civil war broke out in December 2013, when President Salva Kiir Mayardit accused former Deputy President Riek Machar of wanting to carry out a coup. Machar denied the allegations and joined the Sudan People's Liberation Movement-In Opposition (SPLM - IO). Fighting broke out between the SPLM- IO and government forces leading to a full-scale civil war. Ugandan forces have been battling with South Sudanese government forces to bring down the SPLM-IO. The war ended on 22 February 2020 when Kiir and Machar signed an agreement to form a coalition government.[40]

China became involved in the South Sudanese civil war to protect its oil interests. Weapons were sold to government forces to repel attacks on rebel groups. Rebel groups opposed China's exploration and exploitation of oil in the Darfur region and sabotaged Chinese facilities and plants. It also happened that some of the weapons also ended up in the hands of rebel groups. In the period 2011-2013, CQ assault rifles were sold to South Sudan. The Type CQ 5.56x45 assault rifle is a variant of the American M16 rifle.

In 2014, NORINCO supplied more than 1000 tons of weapons and ammunition to the South Sudanese government. The shipment was worth millions of USD and included ground-to-air defense missiles, automatic rifles, grenade launchers, 20000 grenades, hundreds of pistols, machine guns and several million rounds of ammunition.[41]

According to the shipping documents and other relevant information, the huge cargo was loaded in two batches on the Hong Kong registered container ship Feng Huang Song. The ship left the Chinese port of Dalian on May 8 and loaded further supplies at the port of Zhanjiang on May 15, 2014. The port of Mombassa was the final destination. The cargo was then loaded on trucks and transported to the South Sudanese city of Juba.[42]

NORINCO shipped the material under contracts concluded in 2011 and 2013. The transfer of the material was legal, given the absence of an arms embargo against South Sudan at that time. The weapons and ammunition used by the SPLA for the period 2013-2014 were largely of Chinese origin. This is especially true for 7.62x39 patterns (AK variant). Between 2012 and 2014, less than 2 percent of ammunition in the civil war was of Chinese origin, but by the end of 2017 more than half of all 7.62x39mm cartridges were manufactured in China.[43]

The rest of the consignment included the following light weapons and ammunition: 9574 type AK56 automatic assault rifles based on the Russian AK-47/ AKM. Production of the AK56 began in 1956 at Chinese state-owned arms factory 66, but was gradually handed over to NORINCO and Polytechnologies (Polytech). 20 million 7.62x39mm rounds accompanied the AK56s. Also, 2394 LG5 40mm semi-automatic grenade launchers, accompanied by 40x53mm NATO or 40x53mm BGJ-5 grenades.

Also 20000 BGL2 anti-personnel grenades, 319 type 80 machine guns based on the PKM, accompanied by 2 million 7.62x54mm rounds. The Type 80 is a machine gun manufactured since 1980 for infantry training. The specialized, export version of the type 80 is the CF06/LM4, which uses the 7.62x54mm round and has been manufactured since 2008.[44]

Also, 319 type 69-1 rocket powered projectile launchers (RPGs) and 40000 highly explosive projectiles (This is the same type delivered to Sudan). The Type 69-1 is designed to be mounted under the barrels of assault rifles.[45] Also,

660 NP-42 semi-automatic pistols, which is a redesign of the QSZ-92 model and export version. The pistol shoots the 9x19mm parabellum round and has an overall lifespan of 10000 rounds. The pistols were accompanied by 2 million 9x19mm rounds.[46] Other weapons sold by NORINCO to South Sudan include 100 HJ-73D anti-tank missile launchers and 9 simulators. The value of all these weapons and ammunition was 14.5 million USD.

The HJ-73D is a cloned version of the Russian AT-3 Sagger. The missile has been manufactured since 1979 and has a proven track record on the battlefield. Its double warhead has the ability to pierce thick armour and is accurate from 500 to 3000 meters. According to reports, the missile was used against the SPLM rebel group in close contacts.[47]

The 2013 contract also included a consignment of VT2 type 96 tanks. The Type 96 is a second generation combat tank that has been manufactured since 1997 and is almost identical to China's third generation combat tank. The VT-2 made its debut in 2012 and is the export version of the Type 96 series. The tanks arrived at the port of Mombassa on 28 December 2014.

Despite the large consignment of 2014, China continued to supply ammunition to South Sudan. In 2016, Amnesty International reported that the South Sudanese National Intelligence Service (SSNID) used Chinese ammunition in contacts with rebel groups in Luri, on the outskirts of Juba. Heeding to calls from civic society groups and foreign observers that the escalation of foreign weapons is responsible for the continuing violence and loss of life, the UN Security Council in 2016 proposed a ban on the import of weapons to South Sudan. The arms embargo was imposed in 2018 under Resolution 2428, but not without opposition from China and Russia.[48]

The SPLA attempted to use the party-army model of Mao Zedong to strengthen relations between the party and military. A wrong interpretation of the model, however, led to the leadership dispute between President Salva Kiir and Vice President Riek Machar and infighting in the Politburo. The question was whether the party or the military should rule the country? More than half of the Politburo's members were military officers. At a meeting held on 13 December 2013, the differences between the party and military were revealed when the majority of military officers sided with Machar. Machar was then elected interim president.

The Office of Political and Moral Orientation in South Sudan uses the Deputy Chief of Staff to advocate the political ideology of the SPLM/A among military officers. This office follows the same approach as the PLA's Political Department and Uganda's Political Commissariat to earn the loyalty of military personnel to the party.

The role that the political commissioner plays in Mao's model is well executed in Uganda. The Chief Political Commissioner is responsible for training commissioners across the country. Every region in Uganda has a commissioner who reports to the chief political commissioner. Mao's ideology also serves as a guide to unite the ideals of the National Resistance Movement (NRM) and the military.[49] Several members of the NRM were trained by FRELIMO in the war tactics of Mao.

The government of Uganda's regard for Mao is found in military doctrines, manuals and the book "Mission to Freedom". This book was written by President Yoweri Museveni and describes in detail the NRA's freedom struggle. During a visit to Mao's hometown of Hunan in

China, Museveni stated that revolutionaries come to Hunan like Catholics go to Rome.[50]

Tanzania

Mwalimu Julius K. Nyerere and Mao Zedong, both founding members of their respective countries, signed a diplomatic relationship in 1964. China offered to build the Tanzania-Zambia railway (TAZARA) in the early 1970s, after Western countries were not interested in the deal. The completion of TAZARA showed that China was willing to invest in Africa's infrastructure and help African economies develop. This railway line was the first major infrastructure project China completed in Africa.

A former president of Tanzania, HE Benjamin W. Mkapa, stated that relations between the two countries are formed at government and interpersonal level. Citizens from China and Tanzania address each other as friends (Rafiki in Kiswahili) on the street. According to the president, there is no better relationship between Chinese and Africans than in Tanzania.[51]

Every year, the Tanzania People's Defense Forces (TPDF) send troops and officers to China for training. Between 2006 and 2018, more than 500 TPDF members received training in China. Several Chinese instructors also provide training at the TPDF's military school in Dar Es Salaam. Chinese engineers, technical experts and other specialists reside in Dar Es Salaam and are responsible for the repair of aircraft, vehicles and military equipment. The staff is relieved on a rotating basis. Visits by high-level military delegates between the two countries are an indication of the strong military relationship.

The Chinese Navy's Vice Admiral Ai Ping personally intervened to appropriate funds for new coast guard vessels. Servicemen from China's navy trained the operators of these boats. The new coast guard vessels can assist in combating piracy off the Tanzanian coast. In 2016, Defense Minister Shamsi Vuai Nahodh visited China to express his appreciation for the military assistance China is providing.[52]

A new training center for the TPDF was launched in 2018 by John Magafull, the Tanzanian president. The center was funded by the Chinese government at a cost of 30 million USD. It was built in the coastal town of Mapinga and has some of the best training facilities of any military in Africa.[53]

In 2014, joint naval exercises between China and Tanzania were held, the first of its kind since the two countries established diplomatic relations. China has been supplying various military hardware to Tanzania over the years. In 2003, two Y-8 military cargo planes were delivered, in 2007, four ZFB-05 armored troop carriers, in 2011, 30 type 59G tanks, in 2012, 14 F-7MG fighter jets, 6 K-8 flight simulators, and 10 WZ-551 APCS, 24 type 63A light amphibious tanks, 12 type 07PA 120mm self-propelled mortars, FB-6A short range air defense systems and A100 300mm rocket launchers. Two warships, TNS Mwitongo (P77) and TNS Msoga (P78) were delivered by Poly Technologies in 2015. The ships are used to combat illegal fishing and piracy. The Chinese government also built the Tanzanian Military Academy (TMA) and new barracks with room for 12000 officers and troops.[54]

Zambia

The Chinese government has been offering military loans worth 1.5 billion USD to African countries since 2012. These loans are used to buy new equipment, construct new facilities and upgrade existing facilities. The major financial institutions offering the loans are China's

National Development Bank and the Import and Export Bank (Exim). The Aviation Industry Corporation of China (AVIC) and Polytech also make financial contributions to export arms to Africa.

From these loans, it is interesting to note that 40% (600 million USD) are allocated to Zambia, a country with an annual defense budget of about 220 million USD. This raises the question, why such a huge amount is allocated to Zambia. The country is not involved in a civil war, has no civil unrest and no external security threats. The DRC and Sudan, which also receive huge loans from China, are embroiled in civil wars and experience high levels of civil unrest. Given the unstable political situations in the DRC and Sudan, it makes sense for China to provide large loans to a stable country like Zambia. Zambia is a country without a coastline and is not a focal point for China's geostrategic ambitions in Africa.[55]

According to the President of Zambia, the purchase of Chinese weapons is based on the willingness of banks to provide loans. It is unmatched by Italy and Russia, the other arms suppliers to Zambia. Every Chinese aircraft delivered to Zambia was purchased with financial support. Either in the form of Exim bank loans or in the form of

AVIC's credit supply lines. The provision of credit by AVIC allows Zambia to receive the aircraft immediately, but to pay later. Eximbank, on the other hand, is a politically motivated policy bank. Eximbank strives to advance China's strategic interests through foreign investment and international cooperation. Officers in the Zambian military are also impressed with the easy handling of Chinese weapons and low maintenance cost. China is not really interested in how many weapons Zambia buys and for what purpose it is used. These are purely financial transactions for profit.[56]

In 2013, elephant tusks worth 140000 USD were confiscated from a Zambian military officer, who was on route to China for a training session. The officer was arrested at Kenneth Kaunda International Airport in the company of two Chinese embassy officials. The case was thrown out of court because of a lack of evidence. Further investigation revealed that the elephant tusks were exchanged for a consignment of military hardware. Three months, after this incident, Chinese Ambassador Zhou Yuxiao announced a military deal worth 8 million USD.[57]

In April 2014, the Zambian air force placed an order for the delivery of 6 Chinese fighter jets worth USD 100 million. The aircraft were all delivered by the end of 2017. According to a report by the Transparency International Government Defense Anti-Corruption Index Report of February 2015, there is a high risk of corruption in the Zambian military. The report launched an investigation into the military's involvement in the exchange of animal products for financial gain. The report also point out illegal transactions between military officials and diplomats from the Chinese embassy to export ivory to China.[58]

New aircraft, light assault weapons and ammunition were purchased after 2014. The procurement of river patrol boats is an addition to Zambia's new Military Marine Commando Force. From 2015, the following commercial and military aircraft have been delivered to Zambia. These include, the Xian MA60 turbocharged regional aircraft, Z-9 military helicopters, and Hongdu JL-8 multipurpose light training and combat aircraft. The aircraft are all manufactured by AVIC. This company is state-funded and is one of the China's largest aircraft manufacturers.

The Zambian Air Force (ZAF), has been building new facilities and upgrading its fleet in the last decade. New runways, terminals, workshops and training facilities are built to accommodate the expansion of the air force. AVIC supplies most of the ZAF's aircraft and orders have increased in the last 5 years. During an air show in Lusaka in 2017, most of the aircraft that participated were models of AVIC. According to military officials, the ZAF is very proud of the aircraft they purchase from AVIC.[59]

Zimbabwe

China provided military assistance to Zimbabwe during the freedom struggle.[60] The freedom struggle was fought from 1964 until independence on April 18, 1980. Arms and ammunition were supplied to ZANLA, the military wing of ZANU-PF.[61] ZANLA fighters were trained in guerilla warfare and insurgency tactics, which was successfully carried out in rural and suburban areas. In the last phases of the freedom struggle, China supplied ZANLA with large quantities of assault weapons and light artillery to carry out its "final" fight for independence.[62] China's supply of weapons to ZANLA gave ZANU an advantage over other rivals, such as, ZAPU, which was supported by Russia. The rivalry was based on control of rural areas and intimidation of the population.

ZANU's victory in the 1980 election was viewed by ZANLA as a victory of the Maoist doctrine of military uprising over the Russian doctrine of guerrilla warfare. Leaders in the ZANU-PF called for stronger relations with China after the party came to power. Mugabe decided to look East after the British government imposed sanctions on his regime. China was a natural partner because of economic and military aid during the liberation years.

China accounted for 39% of Zimbabwe's conventional arms purchases for the period 2000-2011. Military officers are also trained at the headquarters in Harare. In April 2004, a Chinese radar system was installed at Mugabe's mansion in at a cost of 13 million USD. In the same year, Zimbabwe purchased 12 FC-1 fighter jets and 100 military vehicles. The FC-1 is a light, fourth - generation fighter aircraft developed jointly by the Pakistan Aeronautical Complex (PAC) and the Chengdu Aircraft Corporation (CAC). The FC-1 is based on the Russian Mikoyan-Gurevich MiG-21. The MiG-21 was once very popular among third-world countries, but became outdated with the development of new models.[63]

In 2005, 39 military vehicles and 6 K-8 training aircraft were sold to Zimbabwe at a cost of 3 million USD. In 2006, a second order was delivered. A year after delivery, the aircraft started to breakdown due to mechanical failures. The Zimbabwean government then dispatched 55 senior officers to Beijing for a crash-course in aircraft maintenance. Also in 2006, military equipment worth 1.5 million USD was supplied to Zimbabwe.

In 2009, the Zimbabwean air force received 6 fighter jets at a cost of 120 million USD, but at the end of 2011 all the planes were locked in a hangar. No parts were available for maintenance. After this consignment, China stopped selling fighter jets to Zimbabwe. China was concerned that the Zimbabwe's air force inability to maintain fighter planes may negatively affect the selling of planes to other countries in Africa.[64]

At the end of the 1990s, concessions were granted to China to mine in the Marange area. Officers of the Chinese military were appointed as overseers of the mine's activities.

The placement of personnel at mines was a major driver of China's military relationship with Zimbabwe until the late 2000s. This relationship took a different turn in the years that followed. One of exchanging Zimbabwe's rich mineral deposits for Chinese weapons. A comprehensive

---

report by the news agency, Africa Confidential, indicated that some of the best mining concessions, including concessions rich in platinum and gold, were offered to China and Russia in exchange for weapons. The report: "Arms for minerals trades exposed in Zimbabwe", mentioned the names of high-ranking government officials negotiating arms for minerals deals. The names of the Minister of Justice, Emmerson Mnangagwa and the Deputy Minister of Foreign Affairs, Christopher Mutsvangwa were mentioned in the report. The Chinese military and arms manufacturer NORINCO's involvement in the deals attracted the most attention. NORINCO has been supplying arms to African countries for several years.[65]

The following weapons were sold to Zimbabwe between 2014 and 2020. 1) Armored vehicles sold to Zimbabwe or exchanged for minerals, 2) Battle tanks sold to Zimbabwe or exchanged for minerals, 3) Mining Vehicles, 4) Long-range artillery cannons/Howitzers sold to Zimbabwe or exchanged for minerals, 5) Ammunition and light assault weapons, 6) Precision assault weapons and anti-tank missile systems, Anti-riot weapons and equipment-tear gas, 7) four-wheel drive armored vehicles sold to

---

Zimbabwe or exchanged for minerals, 8) Multiple rocket launchers sold to Zimbabwe or exchanged for minerals.[66] The Chinese military in partnership with NORINCO acquired rights for the mining of Platinum in Chegutu, copper rights in Sanyati and rights for the exploration of gold in Chimanimani. This happened after large sums of money were invested in the NORINCO's Zimbabwean partners, Wanbao and Zimbao.

Chinese arms manufacturers also own the majority of shares in the Anjing mine in the Chiadzwa diamond field. According to the Africa Confidential report, the profits made from the diamond sales were not declared for tax purposes.

It is alleged that profits from the diamond mines were used to support ZANU PF's 2009 election campaign. The British media reported in 2010 that officials from the Zimbabwean and Chinese militaries had a meeting with Mugabe to discuss ways to keep him in power. The looting of the Chiadzwa mines and the disbursement of profits to China were part of the talks. Hundreds of Chinese military personnel were stationed in Zimbabwe before the election. They would help the Zimbabwean army in the event of an uprising against the Mugabe government. This offer to

---

help runs counter to the Chinese government's principle of non-interference in the domestic affairs of other countries, especially where political issues are at stake.[67]

In 2009, the Ang Yue container ship left China with a cargo of weapons destined for Zimbabwe. It was in the same year that elections were held in Zimbabwe.

The weapons included AK-47 assault rifles, 3 million rounds of ammunition, 1500 grenade launchers, and 3,000 mortars and mortar launchers. The ship entered the port of Durban on 15 March. After the contents were inspected, dock workers refused to unload the cargo. A diplomatic dispute arose and the case was referred to the Durban High Court. China had no choice but to recall the ship. It is not known if the weapons were finally delivered to Zimbabwe. For the next two years there were no significant military contacts between China and Zimbabwe.[68]

In 2014, China agreed to build Zimbabwe's National Defense College, which placed military relations back on track. The College of Defense was funded by the State Bank of China and built by Chinese workers. The facility is the largest in Zimbabwe and operated by the departments of the PLA, China's Ministry of State Security (MASC), and Zimbabwe's intelligence service.[69]

In 2019, Spotlight Zimbabwe reported that a military base had been built in central Zimbabwe.

The base contains a ground-to-air defense missile system, similar to the one that is found on Woody Island in the South China Sea. China had been in talks with the Zimbabwean government for years to build a permanent military base in the country. The base is primarily for strategic influence in the region and as a logistics and support center for the protection of economic and mining interests.

Mugabe was against the building of the base and argued that the construction of the base and the presence of the Chinese military could jeopardize Zimbabwe's sovereignty. The Minister of Justice, Emmerson Mnangagwa then seized the opportunity and requested China to invest in the diamond mines at Marange and continue building the base. The base has a strategic importance, because it gives China the power to negotiate further arms for minerals deals. It is a collateral in China's bargaining power.

The integration of the military into the political structures of a party is fraught with risks, as the case of Zimbabwe indicates.

In 2017, the Deputy Minister of the Zimbabwean Army, Constantine Chiwenga, accused ZANU-PF of illegally dismissing high-ranking government and military officials. The accusations were aimed directly at Robert Mugabe. Mugabe fired Emmerson Mnangagwa, the vice-president, that led to unrest within the party and army. Mnangagwa was a popular leader among the top military generals. Mugabe wanted to purge the party and military of members who were opposed to his leadership. It was to retain power in the 2018 election. Chiwenga stated that the military has an interest in respecting the wishes of veterans and should not be used as a political pawn by the government. Chiwenga warned that the military might intervene to stop the purge. A day later, the military took control of several state departments.

ZANU-PF's political commissariat, the seat of the party's power, has always been manned by the country's top generals. Mugabe's faction within ZANU-PF accused the military of disobeying the party and disregarding the party's orders. The basic principle of Maoism is that the military must always obey the party's orders. President Mugabe decided to support his wife Grace's faction as the infighting between ZANU-PF members and military generals continued. Grace was a member of ZANU-PF's Politburo and led the G40 faction. The faction sought to replace older members of the party with the younger generation. This also applied to older members of the military who stood in the way of changes in the organizational structure of ZANU-PF. Chiwenga on the other hand, supported Emmerson Mnangagwa to take over the presidency. Several top generals also sided with Mnangagwa. In a vote of the commissariat, Mnangagwa was unanimously elected new president.[70]

Notes

---

[1] The FNLA is a political party and former military organization that fought for Angola's independence. The leader was Holden Roberto. UNITA is the second largest political party in Angola. The party was founded in 1966 as a movement that fought for the independence of Angola. UNITA has received military aid from China, America and South Africa at various stages of the movement's freedom struggle. The MPLA is a left-wing political party in Angola. The MPLA fought against Portuguese colonialism in the Angolan war for independence and defeated UNITA in the Angolan civil war. The party has been in power since 1975. (See Day, Christopher. 2019. *The Fates of African Rebels: Victory, Defeat, and the Politics of Civil War.* Colorado: Lynne Rienner Publishers, Inc).

[2] Miguel, Junior. 2019. *The Formation and Development of the Angolan Military* . UK: AuthorHouse.

[3] Jackson, Steven F. 1995. China's Third World Foreign Policy: The Case of Angola and Mozambique, 1961-93. *The China Quarterly,* 142 (June): 388-422.

[4] eng.chinamil.com.cn.2019. Angola wants to strengthen military cooperation with China. http://eng.chinamil.com.cn/view/2019-06/25/content_9538110.htm

[5] flightglobal.com.2021. World's Air Forces. https://www.flightglobal.com/download?ac=75345

[6] Nantulya, Paul. 2020a. China Promotes Its Party-Military Model in Africa. 28 July. https://africacenter.org/spotlight/china-promotes-its-party-army-model-in-africa/

[7] On 1 August 1964, the DRC gained independence from Belgium. The first president Mobutu Sese Seko changed the name to Zaire (a former name for the Congo River) on October 27, 1971. The change was part of the president's a *authenticité* ideology, which aimed to get rid of colonial names and to give the country a more authentic and unique national identity. The implementation of the 3 Zs (our country Zaire, our river Zaire, our currency Zaire) was an embodiment of the ideology. Mobutu's call that all citizens wear the Chinese style tunic or uniform of Mao Ze Dong was an indication of his ties with the Chinese government. Mobutu, however, was anti-communist and forged economic relations for economic reasons. The 3 Zs were abolished with the inauguration of Laurent-Désiré Kabila in 1997. (Young, Crawford, and Thomas Turner. 2013. *The Rise and Decline of the Zairian State* . Wisconsin: University of Wisconsin Press).

[8] Young and Turner. 2013. *The Rise and Decline of the Zairian State.*

[9] FARDC is the national military of the DRC. The military consists of various military factions and is one of the most unstable armies in the world (see Day 2019).

[10] Nzongola-Ntalaja. 1979. The Continuing Struggle for National Liberation in Zaire. *The Journal of Modern African Studies,* 17 (4): 595-614.

[11] Banana is located in a cove at the mouth of the Congo River. The inlet is about 1km wide, on the northern bank of the river and separated from the ocean by a land mass of 3km long and 400m wide. It is connected by an 8km long tarred road to the nearest large town of Muanda (see Dipiazza, Francesca D. 2007. *Democratic Republic of Congo in Pictures*. Minneapolis: Twenty-First Century Books).

[12] The LRA is an extremist, religious and terrorist group active in the northern parts of Uganda, South Sudan, the Central African Republic (CAR) and the DRC. The group was founded during the Ugandan Civil War in 1987 by Joseph Kony. The group's goal is to establish a Christian, national government in Uganda. The FDLR is an armed rebel group in the eastern DRC. The members are from the Hutu ethnic group and one of the last factions of Rwandan rebel groups active in the Congo. The M23 was a rebel group active in the eastern parts of the DRC, mainly in the province of Kivu.
The group was responsible for the massacre of thousands of civilians in the DRC. In 2013, the group was defeated by Congolese and UN troops in an attack on their base in Goma. A peace agreement was subsequently signed, which also meant the end of M23 (see Day 2019).

[13] Mbandaka is the capital of the DRC's Equatorial Province and is located on the banks of the Congo River.

[14] Omayundu, Jean-Jaques W. 2018. Joseph Kabila continues to over-equip his regime militarily for the upcoming political deadlines. 23 May. https://afridesk.org/en/joseph-kabila-continues-to-over-equip-his-regime-militarily-for-the-upcoming-political-deadlines-jj-wondo/

[15] Perrett, Bryan. 2004. *Gunboat! Small Ships at War* . Brighton: Cassell.

[16] Omayundu, Jean-Jaques W. 2018. Joseph Kabila continues to over-equip his regime militarily for the upcoming political deadlines.

[17] Shinn, David, 2012. China's Involvement in Mozambique. https://intpolicydigest.org/china-s-involvement-in-mozambique/

[18] Roque, Paula C. 2009. *China in Mozambique: A Cautious Approach Country Case Study*. Braamfontein: South African Institute of International Affairs, Occasional Paper 23: 1-20.

[19] Shinn, 2012. China's Involvement in Mozambique.

[20] Wang, Hejun. 2020. China-Mozambique cooperation yields numerous benefits. 12 November. https://www.globaltimes.cn/content/1206694.shtml

[21] Nantulya, Paul. 2020a. China Promotes Its Party-Military Model in Africa.

[22] Natsios, Andrew S. 2012. China in Sudan: The Challenge of Non-Interference in a Failed State. *Georgetown Journal of International Affairs,* 13 (2): 61–67.

[23] Holt, PM and MW Daly. 2011. The Era of Jaafar Nimeiri: 1969–85. London: Routledge.

[24] Patey, Luke. 2014 . *The New Kings of Crude: China, India, and the Global Struggle for Oil in Sudan and South Sudan* . London: C Hurst & Co Publishers Ltd.

[25] hrw.org.1998. Arms Transfers to the Government of Sudan. https://www.hrw.org/legacy/reports98/sudan/Sudarm988-05.htm#P573_99846

[26] Hoeffel, Joseph M. 2014. *The Iraq Lie: How the White House Sold the War* . San Diego: Progressive Press.

[27] Flint, Julie and Alexander de Waal. 2005. *Darfur: A short history of a long war.* London: Zed Books.

[28] The National Islamic Front (NIF) was an Islamic political organization founded in 1976 and led by Dr. Hassan al-Turabi. The NIF influenced Sudanese politics from 1979 until the late 1990s. The organization was only one of two Islamic movements that gained political power in the 20th century (The other movement was the Islamic Republic of Iran led by Ayatollah Ruhollah Khomeini in 1979) (see Day 2019).

[29] Flint and the Wall. 2005. *Darfur: A short history of a long war.*

[30] africaintelligence.com.1995. OAU Warns Khartoum. https://www.africaintelligence.com/eastern-and-southern-africa/1995/12/23/oau-warns-khartoum,34903-art

[31] flightglobal.com.2021. World's Air Forces. https://www.flightglobal.com/download?ac=75345

[32] Chamberlain, Peter. 1975. Mortars and rockets. New York: Arco Publishing.

[33] army-guide.com.2020. Type 75. http://www.army-guide.com/eng/product4159.html

[34] hrw.org.1998. Arms Transfers to the Government of Sudan.

[35] Williams, Paul. 2016. *War and Conflict in Africa 2nd Edition* . Cambridge: Polity.

[36] Leff, Jonah and Emile LeBrun. 2014. *Following the Thread: Arms and Ammunition Tracing in Sudan and South Sudan* . Switzerland: Graduate Institute of International and Development Studies.

[37] amnestie.org.2012. Darfur: New weapons from China and Russia fuelling conflict. https://www.amnesty.org/en/latest/news/2012/02/darfur-new-weapons-china-and-russia-fuelling-conflict/

[38] The SLM, SLA or SLM/A is an active rebel group in Darfur. The group was founded as the Darfur Liberation Front by members of the Fur, Zaghawa and Masalit ethnic groups. The Justice and Equality Movement (JEM) is a militant group

involved in the conflict in Darfur. The group fought with the SLM against government forces and the Janjaweed for the end of the conflict in Darfur. (see Day 2019).

[39] Leff, Jonah and Emile LeBrun. 2014. Following the Thread: Arms and Ammunition Tracing in Sudan and South Sudan.

[40] bbc.com.2020. South Sudan rivals Salva Kiir and Riek Machar strike unity deal. https://www.bbc.com/news/world-africa-51562367

[41] Mizokami, Kyle. 2021. The Norinco CQ: How Does China's Cloned M16 Hold Up? https://nationalinterest.org/blog/reboot/norinco-cq-how-does-china%E2%80%99s-cloned-m16-hold-181860

[42] amnesty.org. 2014. UN: South Sudan arms embargo crucial after massive Chinese weapons transfer. https://www.amnesty.org/en/latest/news/2014/07/un-south-sudan-arms-embargo-crucial-after-massive-chinese-weapons-transfer/

[43] conflictarm.com.2018. Weapon Supplies into South Sudan's Civil war.https://www.conflictarm.com/reports/weapon-supplies-into-south-sudans-civil-war/

[44] modernfirearms.net.2016. NORINCO LG5 / LG5s / QLU-11 Sniper Grenade Launcher (China). https://modernfirearms.net/en/grenade-launchers/china-grenade-launchers/norinco-lg5-qlu-11-eng/

[45] un.org.2015. Interim report of the Panel of Experts on South Sudan established pursuant to Security Council resolution 2206 (2015) https://www.un.org/ga/search/view_doc.asp?symbol=S/2015/656

[46] Tiezzi, Shannon. 2015. UN Report: China Sold $ 20 Million in Arms and Ammunition to South Sudan. 27 August. https://thediplomat.com/2015/08/un-report-china-sold-20-million-in-arms-and-ammunition-to-south-sudan/

[47] Nkala, Oscar. 2014. South Sudan takes delivery of Chinese infantry weapons. 15 July. https://www.defenceweb.co.za/land/land-land/south-sudan-takes-delivery-of-chinese-infantry-weapons/

[48] amnesty.org.2020. South Sudan: Evidence of violations and illicit concealment of arms must spur UN to renew arms embargo. 30 April. https://www.amnesty.org/en/latest/news/2020/04/south-sudan-evidence-of-violations-and-illicit-concealment-of-arms-must-spur-un-to-renew- arms-embargo/

[49] The NRM was founded as a liberation movement and took power in 1986. The movement brought stability, security, law and order and a new constitution to the country, thus ushering in a new era in Uganda's political direction. (see Day, 2019. The Fates of African Rebels: Victory, Defeat, and the Politics of Civil War).

[50] mediacentre.go.ug.2019. Chairman Mao Liberated China by Clarity of Thought and Strategy "- Museveni. 28 June. https://www.mediacentre.go.ug/media/%E2%80%9Cchairman-mao-liberated-china-clarity-thought-and-strategy%E2%80%9D-%E2%80%93-museveni

[51] globalsecurity.org.2018. Tanzania - China Relations https://www.globalsecurity.org/military/world/tanzania/forrel-prc.htm

[52] The Tanzania People's Defense Force (TPDF) is the military of the United Republic of Tanzania. The TPDF was founded in 1964 after the previous colonial power (the Tanganyika Rifles) broke up. Unlike other African countries, Tanzania has never had a coup or civil war. (see Day 2019).

[53] defenseweb.co.za.2018. Chinese-built military training center opens in Tanzania. https://www.defenceweb.co.za/land/land-land/chinese-built-military-training-centre-opens-in-tanzania/

[54] sipri.org.2019. Trends in International Arms Transfers. https://www.sipri.org/sites/default/files/2019-03/fs_1903_at_2018_0.pdf

[55] Hwang, Jyhjong. 2020. Logics of Arms Deals: Multilevel Evidence from China-Zambia Relations. https://static1.squarespace.com/static/5652847de4b033f56d2bdc29/t/5f4e6eb43420ff01a7240433/1598975678736/WP+37+-+Hwang+-+Zambia+Air+Forces.pdf

[56] Nyabiage, Jevans. 2020. China-Africa arms trade: Zambia largest recipient of Chinese loans for military gear, study says. https://www.scmp.com/news/china/diplomacy/article/3103973/china-africa-arms-trade-zambia-largest-recipient-chinese-loans

[57] Nkala, Oscar. 2016. Chinese-military axis behind Zambian poaching crisis. https://earthjournalism.net/stories/chinese-military-axis-behind-zambian-poaching-crisis

[58] government.defenceindex.org.2015. Zambia. http://government.defenceindex.org/countries/zambia/

[59] lusakatimes.com.2019. Special Forces advanced training pass out parade in Pictures. September 30. https://www.lusakatimes.com/2019/09/30/special-forces-advanced-training-pass-out-parade-in-pictures/

[60] The ZANU was a military organization that fought against the white minority government of Ian Smith. The freedom struggle was known as the Rhodesian Bush War. The organization seceded from the ZAPU in 1975. The split led to factions loyal to Mugabe and factions loyal to Ndabaningi Sithole. Mugabe formed the militant ZANU-PF and Sithole the moderate ZANU-Ndonga party. ZANU-PF has been in power since 1980. (See Day, Christopher. 2019. The Fates of African Rebels: Victory, Defeat, and the Politics of Civil War).

[61] The ZANLA was the military wing of ZANU during the Rhodesian bush war. (see Day, 2019. The Fates of African Rebels: Victory, Defeat, and the Politics of Civil War).

[62] Alao, Abiodun. 2012. *China and Zimbabwe: The Context and Contents of a Complex Relationship. Braamfontein* . South African Institute of International Affairs. Occasional Paper 202.

[63] pac.org.pk.2021. JF-17 Thunder Aircraft. https://www.pac.org.pk/jf-17

[64] Shinn, David H and Joshua Eisenman. 2012. *China and Africa: A Century of Engagement* . Pennsylvania. University of Pennsylvania Press.

[65] africa-confidential.com.2013. Arms for Minerals. December 4th. https://www.africa-confidential.com/article-preview/id/5142/Arms-for-minerals_trades_exposed_

[66] Vassiliou, Chris. 2020. China's Strong Military Presence in Zimbabwe embeds itself in Central / Southern Africa. https://www.linkedin.com/pulse/chinas-strong-military-presence-zimbabwe-embeds-itself-vassiliou/

[67] Malone, Andrew. 2010. Mugabe's darkest secret: An £ 800bn blood diamond mine he's running with China's Red Army. https://www.dailymail.co.uk/news/article-1313123/Robert-Mugabes-darkest-secret-An-800bn-blood-diamond-run-Chinas-Red-Army.html

[68] Alao, 2012. China and Zimbabwe: The Context and Contents of a Complex Relationship.

[69] The Ministry of State Security (MSF) is China's civil, intelligence, security and police agency charged with counter-intelligence, foreign intelligence and political security (Eftimiades, Nicholas. 2017. *Chinese Intelligence Operations: Espionage Damage Assessment Branch* . Washington, US Defense Intelligence Agency: Routledge).

[70] Kingsley, Patrick and Jeffrey Moyo. 2019. A Coup Offered Hope to Zimbabwe. Has Its New President Delivered? 10 August. https://www.nytimes.com/2019/08/10/world/africa/zimbabwe-president-emmerson-mnangagwa-mugabe.html

Chapter 9: Conclusion

China's security policy in Africa follows a two-pronged approach. The first is the protection of the country's economic and security interests and secondly the expansion of its influence in Africa. Many contributions are made to existing multilateral institutions, such as the AU, FOCAC, and regional organizations. The country is participating in peacekeeping missions and UN-sponsored operations to curb terrorism on the east coast of Africa. Both approaches offer China the opportunity to deploy its massive blue water fleet in operational conditions, to be present in the Indian Ocean and to maintain the country's first overseas military base in Djibouti.

China is also building stronger military relations with African countries through diplomatic channels, training, joint military exercises and the construction of military infrastructure. Furthermore, The Chinese military exerts more aggressive and assertive international behaviour by taking part in military operations away from home.

The majority of African governments buy low-cost Chinese weapons that are mostly used to strengthen national security and deployed in conflict situations.

However, the sale of arms to African countries tends to exacerbate conflict and does not contribute to peace and security. While China sells a relatively large number of weapons to countries with an abundance of natural resources, there are countries like Ghana and Uganda, which have few resources and still maintain strong military ties with China. This means that China is using arms sales as a means to make commercial profits. Chinese weapons are used in many of Africa's conflicts. During the Darfur war, China sold arms to both government and rebel forces.

These weapons were responsible for the murder of thousands of civilians. However, China deployed hundreds of troops to the UNMISS to maintain peace between the armed groups. During the conflict between Ethiopia and Eritrea, China sold arms to both governments, while only a few observers were sent to the UNMEE.

Furthermore, China provided weapons to government and rebel forces in the DRC, while troops were deployed to the MONUC at the same time. The mandate of MONUC provided for disarmament, demobilization and repatriation. However, there is little evidence that Chinese troops carried out any of these tasks successfully. While China is not the only country deploying peacekeeping troops and at the same time selling weapons to combat groups, Chinese weapons are used in Africa wars leading to large-scale bloodshed. Chinese companies doing business in Ivory Coast, Liberia and Sierra Leone are accused of smuggling small arms and ammunition to rebel groups and mercenaries. In this way, the conflicts are prolonged. The illicit trade in arms in no way contributes to peace and development.

While cooperation with China appears to be mutually beneficial, African governments need to do more to define their collective interests. The AU as a collective representative of Africa's interests must bear more responsibility to negotiate maximum benefits for Africa.

China is committed to establishing friendly and diplomatic relations with all countries in Africa. Greater involvement in Africa's security not only indicates China's pursuit of peace and security, but also the strategic goal of creating a sphere of influence on the continent. The concept of a community with a shared future should integrate economic, technological, scientific, cultural and security cooperation.

China's long-standing principle of non-interference in the domestic affairs of other countries is less static than before. Nowhere is the principle more challenged than in Africa, where the protection of Chinese citizens is currently considered one of the top security objectives and the government has intervened militarily in Sudan, Libya, the DRC and Somalia to evacuate civilians. If China continues to be economically active in unstable and insecure countries in SSA, it will be difficult to draw a line between the principle of non-interference, economic interests and the protection of citizens.

In the face of security challenges, Chinese leaders have no choice but to adjust the country's Africa policy to meet certain security demands. Non-interference is a key principle of China's foreign policy and crucial to maintaining core interests, especially the survival of the CCP and the protection of Chinese territorial integrity and sovereignty.

It is unlikely that China will stop maintaining a security presence in Africa and will continue to use diplomatic instruments to build peace and security. These include

---

negotiations in various forums, military diplomacy, the provision of services by security contractors and the signing of strategic partnerships. One of the biggest challenges is to find a balance between the nature and extent of security issues and solutions.

China's military presence in Africa poses challenges for several other countries. One of the countries is America, which established AFRICOM in 2007 and is competing with China for military influence. This include the training of soldiers and the provision of military equipment. The presence of the base in Djibouti also increases China's ability to gather intelligence on US military involvement. By the end of 2020, America was still the largest financial contributor to peacekeeping missions, but runs the risk of unknowingly funding China for the peacekeeping missions. China's willingness to sell arms to Sudan and South Sudan runs counter to UN sanctions and undermines America's efforts to address human rights abuses in these countries. The possibility also exists that Chinese weapons could exacerbate conflict in the countries.

China's continued investment in Africa's ports, specifically ports that can be used for military and commercial use, increases the possibility that China may build more bases in Africa.

The AU and regional organization's call to China for the promotion of peace and security are having a positive impact. China supports the protocol of the AU's peace and security architecture and deploy troops to the AU's standing force. Furthermore, China's contributions to peacekeeping missions are viewed in a positive light and much work has already been carried out to build peace. China supports the application of law and order by qualified UN police officers in situations where human rights abuses take place. Staff are also trained to assist in humanitarian crises. Recent examples are assistance in the provision of Covid-19 vaccine and efforts to control the Ebola virus in the DRC.

China's increased involvement in Africa's security will inevitably lead to a consolidation of military agreements and more arms deals. This is on a continent where conflict, social and workplace inequalities, and bad government are the order of the day. The absence of law and order, a continuation of civil wars and other forms of civil strife are also common.

China is likely to continue to pursue a multidimensional approach to security in Africa. This approach combines participation in peacekeeping missions, the upkeeping of the Djibouti base, the provision of financial and logistical support to African armies, the maintaining of military diplomacy and the deployment of security contractors. These dimensions all point to the execution of influence and building stronger relations with African governments. Of course, geo-economic and geo-strategic goals are also important. Finally, the signing of military agreements and strategic partnerships point to the strengthening of African countries' military capacity and the protection of Chinese interests and citizens.

Index